PRAISES FOR

GETTING THE CHURCH INSIDE YOU

Steven Parker has accomplished a rare feat with his accessible, practical study of Ephesians. Drawing on his decades of experience as a pastor and student of scripture, he combines the best of contemporary biblical scholarship with real-life examples of the pain, joy, trauma, and blessing of the Christian journey. The result is a commentary that pays attention to the context in which the Letter to the Ephesians was written and the context of contemporary readers. The chapter on spiritual warfare, in particular, is one of the most careful and nuanced treatments I have ever read. In an age when the divisions in church and society can seem insurmountable, Parker's study encourages us to recover what unites us in Christ. Ideal for adult education settings or personal study, this is a book that will serve the church well for many years to come.

—**David H. Jensen**, Professor in the Clarence N. and Betty B. Frierson Distinguished Chair of *Reformed Theology, Austin Seminary*

***

In a consistently changing church culture, it's refreshing to be reminded of the simplicity of what it biblically means to be "the church." This book gives a theological and yet practical approach from Paul's letter to the Ephesians. Steven writes in an encouraging and yet challenging way for the saint of God to both remember and practice what it means to be part of God's greater story for us. As Christians, our personal life is not separate from church life. They go together! We are the church, and this book reminds us of that very fact!

—**Sammy Lopez**, national speaker, content writer, and Teaching Pastor in *Orlando, FL*

***

In our post-pandemic world, Dr. Steven Parker offers fresh and powerful insight from Ephesians that meets the reader at the intersection of incorporating biblical truth into daily living during uncertain times. Parker masterfully illustrates many of his themes through personal experiences from his years of ministering and walking alongside the people of God as they navigate their life journeys. This book delivers practical and invaluable ways to begin balancing what we believe as Christ followers, understanding the grace needed to "flesh" it out in the marketplace so others can see the transforming power Jesus makes in our lives.

—**Joe Rangel, Ph.D.**, Director, *George W. Truett Seminary, San Antonio*

***

In this "must-read" book, Steven Parker provides a path leading to the intersection of God's purpose, plan, and practice for believers. Warning: your life may change after reading Parker's walk through Ephesians.

—**Gus Reyes, PhD**, Director, *Hispanic Partnerships, Dallas Baptist University*

***

Steven Parker offers a faithful and pastorally sensitive reading of Ephesians, balancing exegetical depth with practical application. *Getting the Church Inside You: Balancing Faith and Action* is an accessible contribution to the ongoing conversation about the role of the church in God's redemptive mission.

—**Jonathan L. Smith D.Min., C.C.C., C.R.C.**, Director, *Church Health and Growth, Texas Baptists (Baptist General Convention of Texas)*

Getting the Church Inside You

Balancing Faith and Action

A Narrative Study of Ephesians

Steven K. Parker

Published by KHARIS PUBLISHING, an imprint of
KHARIS MEDIA LLC.

ISBN-13: 978-1-63746-675-9

ISBN-10: 1-63746-675-7

Library of Congress Control Number: 2026935183

All KHARIS PUBLISHING products are available at special quantity discounts for bulk purchases for sales promotions, premiums, fund-raising, and educational needs. For details, contact:

Kharis Media LLC
Tel: +1 (331) 312-2376
support@kharispublishing.com
www.kharispublishing.com

DEDICATION

I thank God for my children, Morgan, Nathan, Casey, and Micah. Each of you is my favorite and my joy. You have taught me grace, perseverance, and love in ways deeper than you know. I am proud of the people you are becoming, and I thank God daily for the gift you are in my life. I dedicate the words of this book to you.

I give thanks for Lisa, my wife, my best friend, my ride-or-die partner, and the highlight of every chapter we have shared. Your love, support, and faithfulness are the heartbeat of my life and ministry. This book, like every season of my calling, is offered in gratitude for you and belongs to you as much as it belongs to me.

FOREWORD

Pastoring is not glamorous work. You can be forgiven if you think differently. After all, there is plenty of seeming evidence to the contrary. If you open social media and do just a little bit of searching, you will be met with countless Christian "influencers." These accounts—many of them with thousands and thousands of followers—will give you up-to-the-minute thoughts on how the Christian faith and current events relate to one another.

Perhaps inspired by these influencers, churches are more active on social media these days, posting poignant sermon clips from their respective pulpits. As a result, preachers feel more and more pressure to look better and to speak with greater punch in smaller bursts. This is, after all, how sound bites are created. And sound bites are essential in the attention economy.

All of this presses those in church leadership to become "content creators." Podcasts and posts proliferate innumerable words about countless topics to unknown consumers—to those who may or may not be within their (or any) local congregation. The content creators churn out opinions and hot takes as quickly as they can, and the hungering masses eagerly devour them.

And there, in the middle of it all, are those bearing the title of "pastor." Yes, you can be forgiven if you thought of pastoring as glamorous. But what if pastoring is something altogether different? Years ago, in his classic *Working the Angles*, Eugene Peterson lamented the phenomenon of pastors abandoning their posts at an alarming rate. At the time he wrote those words (in the late twentieth century), there was no internet. Social media was yet to be imagined. And yet, even then, pastors were thinking more about fame than they were about faithfulness. We have not changed much. We have always thought of abandoning our posts for something more exciting, something that grabs more attention. All these concerns are why I love this book by Steven Parker. Steven is a pastor in the most traditional of senses: He loves to shepherd and care for the people God has entrusted to him. He serves in a church that you probably haven't heard of in a town you probably haven't heard of, unless you go to his church or live in his town. He probably hasn't been popping up in your social media feed or adjusting your algorithm's way of thinking. Steven has been serving in relative obscurity in a local church in a local community helping real people make their way through real life. And, because of that, he has a real pastoral ministry.

Stories from real pastoral ministry fill the pages of this book. Each one of them made me greatly appreciate the power of presence—a gift that Steven has in abundance. As he spends time with, prays with, teaches, and serves the people under his care, he garners more and more trust from each of them. In doing so, he becomes the sort of pastor who not only loves these people but also cares deeply about the sort of things that might be forming them. Which is why he cares deeply about the church. Steven wants to see a church that is more than a collection of programs. Instead, he wants to see something beautiful and life giving that might penetrate the lives of those under his care, something that will bring the very beauty and power of the gospel of God to bear on the souls of those who must navigate an increasingly complex life. As he read through the full counsel of Scripture, it was no accident that he settled on the message of Paul's letter to the Ephesians as his basis. Paul, too, cared deeply for the people under his care. Paul, too, wanted a church that was something bigger than a large collection of programs. Paul, too, wanted the power of the gospel to enter his people.

Steven walks us through the writings of Pastor Paul, helping us understand the power and the beauty of a church that is fully surrendered to the Way of Jesus. Paul dealt with many of the same issues pastors deal with today: division, racism, theology, and spiritual warfare—just to name a few. Steven shows us how the message of Ephesians is timeless and how the same message that brought healing and wholeness to the people of Ephesus two thousand years ago can bring healing to those of us reading today. If we allow the church to get inside of us, as Steven says, then we can live the sorts of lives that God has planned for us before the foundation of the world.

Enjoy this book. It is the story of a real pastor doing real pastoring in the real world. If you do, I believe you'll find good news for a thirsty soul. It may not be glamorous, but it is very, very good.

Rev. Steve Bezner, Ph.D.

Associate Professor of Pastoral Ministry and Theology
George W. Truett Theological Seminary

ACKNOWLEDGMENTS

Ministry is not a solitary journey. Along the way, God has blessed us with companions, mentors, encouragers, and fellow servants who have walked beside us. We are deeply grateful to each one who has shared in this calling.

We are thankful for the faithful staff team and volunteers at First Baptist Church Weslaco. Your dedication and heart are a blessing, and your friendship and partnership in ministry continue to inspire us.

We give thanks for the wonderful people of First Baptist Church Cotulla. The fruitful years of ministry with you left an indelible mark on our calling.

We cherish our dear friends at Community Baptist Church in Dublin. The season of ministry we shared helped shape our pastoral voice and heart.

We remember with gratitude the people of First Baptist Church Hawley. Your encouragement during our first steps in vocational ministry gave us the foundation we needed to grow.

From Lyford to Weslaco, by way of West Texas, North Texas, and Southwest Texas, every congregation we have served has left a unique and lasting imprint on our life and calling. We pray that by the end of this journey through Ephesians, the church will get inside you too, if it hasn't already.

A teaching guide, chapter introductions, and other resources can be accessed at:

https://www.drstevenparker.com/getting-the-church-inside-you-resources.

CONTENTS

Introduction....19

Prison Epistle of Paul....20

City of Ephesus....22

Circular Letter with a Specific Purpose....24

Chapter 1: A Message of Grace and Peace for the Saints Ephesians 1:1-2....27

From Whom / To Whom....28

A Message for the Saints....31

Spiritual Practice: Fast-Forward Grace....34

Even When We Don't Feel Like "Holy Ones"....34

Grace and Peace to Y'all....36

Chapter 2: A Prayerful Reminder of the Larger Story Ephesians 1:3–23....42

Spiritual Practice: Story Reframing....44

Praise That Reframes Our Perspective....45

Chosen and Adopted by the Father....48

Saved and Redeemed by the Son....50

Sealed by the Spirit....53

Paul's Prayer for the Church....57

Chapter 3: From Death to Life: A Tale of Two Funerals Ephesians 2....62

But God.......63

From Death to Life in Real Time....65

A Resurrection Story Up Close....67

God's Handiwork....68

Spiritual Practice: Walk the Grace Line 70
A New Community 71
Chapter 4: That's My Brother: A Barrier-Defying Gospel Ephesians 3 78
No Longer Jew vs. Greek 80
That's My Brother 83
Spiritual Practice: See the Brother 85
Breakthrough Praise 86
Living Like Heirs 87
Chapter 5: Balancing Our Call and Walk Ephesians 4:1-16 92
Ones and Fives: Finding Balance 92
Axios: A Life of Balance 93
Rich Young Ruler or Zacchaeus: Adjusting a Tilted Scale 97
Gifted for Service 99
Harmony in the Body 102
Avoiding Imbalance: Truth in Love 104
Spiritual Practice: Balance Audit, A Calling and Walk Self-Check 107
Chapter 6: Throwing Off Our Grave Clothes Ephesians 4:17–32 111
Out with the Old, in with the New 112
Renewed Minds, New Desires 113
The New Walk: Living in Resurrection Reality .. 114
Historical and Cultural Background: Ephesus 117
Finding Common Values in Christ 117
A New Wardrobe 118

Spiritual Practice: Putting Off and Putting On ... 122

Chapter 7: Growing Into Our Father's Clothes Ephesians 5:1-21 ... 126

Mimicking Our Heavenly Father ... 128

Christlike Love in Action ... 130

Holy Living ... 132

Spiritual Practice: A Daily Dress Rehearsal ... 134

Living in the Spirit's Light ... 134

Chapter 8: Homes and Workplaces Directed by the Spirit of God Ephesians 5:17–6:10 ... 143

Understanding the Cultural Context ... 145

Lives of God-Honoring Submission ... 146

Wives and Husbands: Spirit-Shaped Marriage ... 147

Parents and Children: Spirit-Shaped Parenting ... 149

Holy Rhythms ... 151

Everyday Submission and Sacrifice: Levity and Grace ... 152

Caring for Yourself as an Act of Preparation for Submission ... 154

A Radically Countercultural Instruction ... 155

Spiritual Practice: Daily Submission ... 156

Being Christlike in Our Workplaces ... 157

Chapter 9: Gearing Up for Spiritual Warfare Ephesians 6:10–17 ... 165

Getting It Wrong in Different Ways ... 167

Identifying Our True Enemy ... 169

Standing Firm ... 173

Wearing the Right Armor ... 174

Spiritual Practice: Suit Up in Prayer 178

Chapter 10: Incorruptible Love: Prayerfully Embodying the Church Ephesians 6:18–23...... 183

A Life of Prayer 186

Spiritual Practice: Embodying the Idea of the Church Through Prayer 190

A Shared Life of Faith 191

Tychicus: A Trusted Messenger 192

Peace, Love, Faith, Grace 196

Epilogue: Let the Church Live Inside You 201

Bibliography 203

INTRODUCTION

One of the great challenges in the Christian life is finding balance, integrating what we believe with how we live. Ephesians, though not Paul's longest letter, may be his clearest expression of that integration. It offers a concise yet powerful summary of the Christian faith[1] while describing God's plan and purpose for the church in both doctrine and daily living.[2]

Eugene Peterson captures this balance between the essential teachings of our faith and the practice of our faith:

> *What we know about God and what we do for God have a way of getting broken apart in our lives. The moment the organic unity of belief and behavior is damaged in any way, we are incapable of living out the full humanity for which we were created. Paul's letter to the Ephesians joins together what has been torn apart in our sin-wrecked world.*[3]

---

[1] Ray Summers, "Ephesians, Letter to The," in the *Holman Illustrated Bible Dictionary*, ed. Chad Brand et al (Nashville, TN: Holman Reference, 2015), 491.

[2] J. B. Bond, "The Epistle of Paul the Apostle to the Ephesians," in *The Grace New Testament Commentary*, ed. Robert N. Wilkin (Denton, TX: Grace Evangelical Society, 2010), 859.

[3] Eugene H. Peterson, *The Invitation: A Simple Guide to the Bible* (Colorado Springs: NavPress, 2008), 179.

As Millard J. Erickson observes, Ephesians is carefully divided into "doctrinal instruction in the first half and practical exhortation in the second," making it one of Paul's richest expressions of belief flowing into behavior.[4] To fully appreciate that balance, we need to know both the man who wrote it and the world in which it was first heard.

Prison Epistle of Paul

The author of this letter was originally known by his Hebrew name, Saul. He was born a Roman citizen in the city of Tarsus. As a young Jewish Pharisee, Saul studied in Jerusalem under Gamaliel, one of the most prominent rabbis of his day. Passionate for his Jewish faith, Saul considered converts to "the Jesus Way"[5] heretics and traveled widely to persecute the early church with fierce determination.

On the road to Damascus, Saul was blinded by a great light, was spoken to by Jesus, and was radically converted to Christianity. The former enemy of the church became its greatest proponent and came to be known by his Greek name, *Paul.* His name means "little" in Greek, a humble title for a man whose

---

[4] Millard J. Erickson, "Ephesians," in *The Evangelical Commentary on the Bible*, ed. Walter A. Elwell (Grand Rapids, MI: Baker Book House, 1989), 1049.

[5] Eugene H. Peterson, *The Jesus Way: A Conversation on the Ways That Jesus Is the Way* (Grand Rapids, MI: Eerdmans, 2007), 3. Peterson uses this phrase regularly throughout the work and here frames "the Jesus Way" as the way Jesus lived, not merely the truth that He taught.

spiritual influence was anything but small. While we may picture Paul as a spiritual giant, early tradition suggests he was physically unimpressive: short, bald, and ordinary.[6] He may have looked more like the man next door than a superhero of the faith. His life reminds us that eternal influence has little to do with outward appearance or worldly success.

Paul traveled across the ancient world with the gospel, leading Jews and Gentiles to faith in Jesus and planting churches. Along the way, he corresponded with these new believers through letters, teaching them about the Christian faith and encouraging them in the face of internal challenges and external persecution. These letters now make up much of our New Testament.

The titles of the New Testament letters were added long after they were written. When the early church unrolled this scroll, it didn't have "Ephesians" printed in bold at the top. Other letters were named for their authors, like 1 and 2 Peter or 1, 2, and 3 John. Paul's letters were named for their recipients, such as 1 and 2 Corinthians or Galatians, because he wrote so many.[7] This makes sense; it would sound odd to invite a congregation to turn in their Bibles to "13th Paul."

---

6 Robert James Utley, *Paul Bound, the Gospel Unbound: Letters from Prison (Colossians, Ephesians and Philemon, Then Later, Philippians)*, vol. 8, Study Guide Commentary Series (Marshall, TX: Bible Lessons International, 1997), 70.

7 John Muddiman, *The Epistle to the Ephesians*, Black's New Testament Commentaries (London: Continuum, 2001), 56.

Ephesians sits alongside Philippians, Philemon, and Colossians as one of Paul's prison epistles, written during his Roman house arrest. Most of us, after a bad day or in a season of hardship, find it difficult to pray or stay spiritually focused. Paul, imprisoned for his faith, turned confinement into a ministry of encouragement through letters. His example teaches us how our struggles can point others toward God's heart and help them on their spiritual journey.

City of Ephesus

Located in what is now western Turkey, Ephesus was considered "the first and greatest metropolis of Asia," with a population of around 250,000.[8] It was the center of Artemis worship, home to the temple of Artemis, one of the seven wonders of the ancient world, which drew thousands of visitors each year. Artemis worship was big business. The priesthood grew wealthy through occult practices and acted as bankers to the Middle Eastern world, issuing large loans to individuals and nations alike.

Magic, witchcraft, and sorcery flourished in Ephesus. The fledgling church there began with small gatherings in homes. Their movement must have seemed insignificant compared to the city's thriving pagan religions, yet God's Spirit was using them to bring hope and meaning to people who were

---

[8] M. G. Easton, *Illustrated Bible Dictionary and Treasury of Biblical History, Biography, Geography, Doctrine, and Literature* (New York, 1893), 232.

discovering that their "successful" religious ventures were empty and lifeless.[9]

The book of Acts records Paul's miracles in Ephesus. Many new believers brought their magic books and burned them publicly. Luke notes that their value totaled "fifty thousand pieces of silver" (Acts 19:19 ESV), roughly the equivalent of $1.1 million in today's currency.[10]

Such conversions created an economic crisis for religious professionals. Idol makers were losing business as people turned from false gods to Christ. One guild leader stirred up a riot that drove Paul from the city, a conflict motivated less by theological debate than by financial loss.

Paul's later reminder still resonates: "For we do not wrestle against flesh and blood, but against the rulers, against the authorities, against the cosmic powers over this present darkness, against the spiritual forces of evil in the heavenly places" (Eph. 6:12 ESV). His teaching on spiritual warfare comes against this backdrop of tension between the church and the pagan systems of the city.

---

[9] Lawrence O. Richards, *The Bible Reader's Companion*, electronic ed. (Wheaton, IL: Victor Books, 1991), 795.

[10] R. C. Sproul, *The Purpose of God: Ephesians* (Fearn, Scotland: Christian Focus Publications, 1994), 11–14. The monetary value for 50,000 *drachmas* is adjusted for inflation.

Circular Letter with a Specific Purpose

Some of the oldest manuscripts of Ephesians do not include a specific audience, and the letter lacks many of the personal details found in Paul's other writings. Many scholars believe it was a circular letter meant to be read in multiple churches across Asia Minor, more like a written sermon than private correspondence. We can imagine it being read aloud with the reader inserting the name of the local church: *"Paul, an apostle of Christ Jesus by the will of God, to the saints who are in (insert the name of your city) and are faithful in Christ Jesus"* (Eph. 1:1).

Many consider Ephesians to be Paul's greatest doctrinal statement in the New Testament. Here, he weaves together salvation, truth, and righteousness into a concise yet comprehensive picture of the Christian calling.[11] He urges believers to grow in grace and to live out that grace in practical ways.[12]

Though the church in Ephesus appeared small, and Paul's imprisonment looked like defeat, the community formed in Christ would ultimately share in God's great victory over the spiritual forces of darkness. This

---

[11] W. C. Fields, "Ephesians," in *The Teacher's Bible Commentary: A Concise, Thorough Interpretation of the Entire Bible Designed Especially for Sunday School Teachers*, eds. H. Franklin Paschall and Herschel H. Hobbs (Nashville: Broadman and Holman, 1972), 745.

[12] W. Harold Mare, *New Testament Background Commentary: A New Dictionary of Words, Phrases and Situations in Bible Order* (Fearn, Scotland: Christian Focus Publications, 2004), 302-3.

triumph would be accomplished through *agape*,[13] the Greek word for "love" that early Christians filled with deep meaning. Paul uses various forms of this word nineteen times in Ephesians, beginning and ending his message with love (Eph. 1:4–6 and Eph. 6:23–24).

God sent Paul with a special message that the good news of Jesus was for everyone. As Harold Hoehner explains, Paul's stewardship of grace was "to make known that Gentiles are fellow heirs, members of the same body, and partakers of the promise in Christ Jesus through the gospel."[14]

The prevailing message of Ephesians is that God's love transforms the world as the church forms a new kind of community, one that is internalized by His people. This letter was written to shape a people, then and now. It calls us to be a community rooted in love and grounded in truth.

As we journey through Ephesians, may its truth shape us into a Spirit-filled community where God's

---

[13] James Strong, *The Exhaustive Concordance of the Bible* (New York: Hunt & Eaton; Cincinnati: Cranston & Stowe, 1890), G26, *agape* (ἀγάπη): love, especially divine love, selfless and sacrificial love that seeks the good of others. It is distinct from other Greek words for love (*eros*: romantic passion; *philia*: friendship or affection; *storgē*: familial bond). For Paul it is the highest Christian virtue (1 Cor. 13:13), seen supremely in Christ's death on the cross (Eph. 5:2).**Future Strong's notes will simply contain the Strong's number, transliteration, Greek word or phrase, and definition and / or lexical information.**

[14] Harold W. Hoehner, *Ephesians: An Exegetical Commentary* (Grand Rapids, MI: Baker Academic, 2002), 462.

love runs deep and where the church doesn't merely surround us, but lives within us.

Chapter 1

A Message of Grace and Peace for the Saints Ephesians 1:1-2

Paul, an apostle of Christ Jesus by the will of God,
To the saints who are in Ephesus, and are faithful in
Christ Jesus: Grace to you and peace from God our
Father and the Lord Jesus Christ.
(Ephesians 1:1-2)

In November 2019, reports of a new virus in China inched closer to home. By mid-March 2020, what once felt distant became all-consuming. COVID-19 shut down schools, businesses, and churches. Our congregation quickly shifted from in-person to online worship and ministry, thanks to a remarkable team of leaders. We conducted parking lot services, living room communion experiences, backyard baptisms, and a host of other ways of "doing church" we'd never considered.

In those uncertain days, we stopped asking how to get people back into church and started asking a better question: How can we get the church inside people?

Even amid global upheaval, we clung to this truth: The gospel of grace and peace holds fast; scattered or gathered, God still speaks, reaches people, and invites us into His work. That conviction drew us to Paul's letter to the Ephesians.

From Whom / To Whom

The opening words in Greek name the sender: Apostle[15] Paul. Once the church's fiercest enemy, Paul pursued followers of Jesus as dangerous heretics. But on the road to Damascus, he encountered Christ, was blinded by light, and was called into a new life. Saul the persecutor became Paul the champion of grace, embarking on a gospel mission that reshaped the early church.

None of that happened by accident or happenstance. Paul makes it clear that he was not a self-appointed apostle. He was "an apostle of Christ Jesus by the will of God" (1:1). God sent him with a special

[15] *G652, apostolos (ἀπόστολος)*: apostle, messenger, one who is sent. It refers to a commissioned representative who carries the authority of the sender. It was used in general Greek for envoys, ships sent out, or authorized agents. In the NT, it refers to those specifically sent out by Christ.

message: the good news of Jesus was for everyone.[16] Paul's conversion and bold ministry reverberated across the ancient world.

Early in this letter to the believers in and around Ephesus, we discover that, even amid seasons of anxiety and struggle, God has something urgent to say to us and he often communicates through unexpected messengers.

- Who feels beyond the gospel's reach?
- How can we share the good news of Jesus with that person?

The next two Greek words declare the important subject of this message from the apostle Paul. He writes to proclaim the name of Christ Jesus. As storms raged around the church, Paul announced the gospel. The Jesus whose followers Paul once persecuted now became the transformational center of Paul's story.

The very message Paul tried to extinguish became the fire at the center of his life and mission. Paul now believed that the God who created the world and everything in it "made himself known in and through Jesus. As far as Paul is concerned, any picture of God which doesn't now have Jesus in the middle of it is a

[16] Harold W. Hoehner, "Ephesians," in *The Bible Knowledge Commentary: An Exposition of the Scriptures*, eds. J. F. Walvoord and R. B. Zuck, vol. 2 (Wheaton, IL: Scripture Press Publications, 1985), 614.

distortion or a downright fabrication."[17] For Paul, there is no gospel apart from Jesus Christ.

As Scot McKnight observes, both Ephesians and Colossians place Jesus Christ at the very center of Paul's life and ministry. In these letters, McKnight writes, "you will come to see that Jesus is Creator, Redeemer, and Sustainer of all creation. In him the fullness of God lives bodily, and he is all the believers needed then and need now."[18] Paul's writings call us to keep our eyes fixed on Jesus Christ, the heart of our faith and the source of our transformation. Once Paul met Jesus, everything changed. He lived to share the grace that set him free.

Paul wanted everyone to know about his Master, Savior, and King. Whatever we glean from this study, the main point is that Paul is drawing us into the gospel story of Jesus, from beginning to end. Jesus Christ is all the good news we could ever need.

---

[17] N.T. Wright, *Paul for Everyone: The Prison Letters: Ephesians, Philippians, Colossians, and Philemon* (London: Society for Promoting Christian Knowledge, 2004), 5.

[18] Scot McKnight, *Ephesians and Colossians: Diversity in Unity*, New Testament Everyday Bible Study Series (Grand Rapids, MI: HarperChristian Resources, 2025), xiii.

A Message for the Saints

Paul addresses this message about Jesus to the saints,[19] the holy ones set apart by God. We might hesitate to use the word "saint" because it feels lofty and out of reach. We often reserve the term for someone unusually devout or patient, perhaps someone who "puts up with a difficult spouse" or performs a miracle. We think of saints as super-Christians.

Paul doesn't reserve the word for spiritual elites. Instead, he speaks it over flawed, ordinary people like us and calls us what God already sees: saints. We can be called "holy ones," not because of remarkable faith, but because of God's remarkable grace.

In fact, *hagios* is Paul's favorite term for Christians. He uses it nine times in Ephesians.[20] Were the believers in Ephesus better Christians than those we encounter at our church on Sundays? Were these believers of the surrounding region of Asia Minor more holy than the hot and cold church members with whom we share life? When Paul uses the word "saint," he's not

---

[19] G40, *hagios* (ἅγιος): holy, set apart, or consecrated. It comes from the root idea of being different, other, or dedicated to the divine. Paul frequently calls believers *ἅγιοι* ("saints") not because of personal perfection but because they are set apart in Christ, belonging to Him.

[20] Eugene Peterson, *Practice Resurrection: A Conversation on Growing Up in Christ* (Grand Rapids, MI: William B. Eerdmans Publishing Company, 2010), Kindle Page 865.

describing perfection but divine designation. God acknowledges something holy in us.

God recognizes something sacred in the ordinary, imperfect, and motley crew of Jesus followers that make up the church. We are saints not because we've earned the title but because God claimed us. Our status as holy ones comes from that state of being chosen.

Jesus followers are saints because of what Jesus has done for us. Yet we often dodge responsibility with, "Well, I'm no saint," as if denying our sainthood lets us off the holiness hook. But if God calls us saints, disregarding that title fails to honor His grace in calling us and His work in setting us apart. That's not something we can just shrug off.

Peterson points out how calling ordinary believers "saints" should create dissonance within us. We know our flaws. We see the mess. But Paul invites us to take a second look, to see ourselves and others not as unfinished projects but as people already set apart in Christ. God is fast-forwarding our story to its holy conclusion.[21]

My good friend Pastor Ray Sanchez once caught himself growing impatient with a church member stuck in a repeated sin struggle. I understood his impatience; walking with believers through faith's ups and downs can be exhausting (I can't help but wonder if God feels that way about me).

---

[21] Peterson, *Practice Resurrection*, Kindle Page 864–912.

Mid-conversation, Ray thought, "Wait a minute, I'm talking to a saint." That shift changed everything. He stopped watching the rough cut of this person's life and caught a glimpse of God's final edit. It was like seeing a preview of the finished film, a moment when the loose threads and clumsy scenes gave way to the beauty of a fully redeemed story. That vision of grace transformed his frustration into compassion. He didn't excuse the mess, but he chose to view it through the lens of what Jesus was still writing. Ray remembered that in Christ, we're all works in progress, but none of us are stuck in the blooper reel forever. God is developing a masterpiece.

Imagine the transformation that might occur if we consistently viewed ourselves and others as Paul did: as saints, set apart by God. That perspective helps us look through the disarray and glimpse what is coming because of what Jesus has done, is doing, and promises to do. Now comes the lifelong journey of growing into that sanctified identity.

- Who is the most annoying person in your church (maybe keep this answer between you and the Lord)?
- How would fast-forwarding the story God is writing in this person to the end impact how you relate to them?

Seeing people as God does is a big step toward getting the church inside you!

Spiritual Practice: Fast-Forward Grace

This week, choose one person you find difficult to love (at home, at work, or in your church). Write that person's name down. Each day, pray for that person by name, asking God to help you see that person not as they are today, but as that person will be when grace has finished its work.

Write a single sentence that imagines that "future grace" version of that person. Something like this: *"She is a woman full of compassion and wisdom."* Or, *"He is a man of peace and humility."*

As you pray, let God's view of that person reshape yours. Try to interact with that person not according to your frustration, but according to the saint they are becoming in Christ.

Even When We Don't Feel Like "Holy Ones"

I once had the privilege of walking a dear friend through the last chapter of his life. He had lived a faithful life, humbly serving the church, extending kindness to others, and quietly embodying the grace of Jesus. He was one of only a few people I've known of whom it could truly be said, "I never heard an unkind word spoken about him." If you didn't like this man, it was because something was wrong with you.

In his final days, I sat beside him in the hospital. Through intense pain and tears, he whispered, "What if I've just been playing a game? What if I don't really have true faith in God?" This saint, whose life overflowed with the fruit of the Spirit, was now unsure of the very faith he had so faithfully lived. He couldn't see what everyone else could.

I took his hand and said, "My friend, if your life of faith has been just a game, then sign me up for it."

We prayed for peace and the presence of Christ to meet him in his suffering. A few days later, he breathed his last. And I'm convinced he heard the words that await the faithful: "Well done, good and faithful servant...enter into the joy of your master" (Matthew 25:21 ESV).

We may not feel like saints. But our feelings don't define us. Jesus does. Our thoughts don't determine our identity. Christ does. He defines us, claims us, and completes the good work He began.

In the introduction, we noted that Ephesians is less a personal letter and more a circulating sermon. It was written to encourage all the churches in and around Ephesus. These believers from the churches of Asia Minor faced opposition and uncertainty but gathered to hear that they were saints. They were set apart by God. That's a message we still need desperately.

Today, we might write the introduction to the letter this way: "Paul, an apostle of Christ Jesus by the will of God, to the saints in [insert your city] who are faithful in Christ Jesus." Personalizing this circulating sermon helps us see that this call to embody the gospel is for our church in our city. Ephesians has a message for us.

As we face our own illnesses, divisions, and seasons of political strife, we can receive this ancient word afresh.

Our progress in holiness may feel painstakingly slow, but God will not fail in His efforts of transformation. Our church may be composed of a bunch of knuckleheads, but God calls it a collection of holy ones. We are not yet what we shall be, but grace has already called us holy and peace has already made a home in our hearts.

Grace and Peace to Y'all

Paul's greeting, "grace[22] and peace,"[23] is more than a formal address. It is not just a two-word pleasantry; it's a condensed description of the gospel. Grace expresses God's unmerited love and kindness. Peace echoes the Hebrew *shalom* of wholeness and rest. Together they form a blessing of good news.

In those words, Paul declares that God's loving favor and abundant life are now freely ours in relationship with Him and His people.[24] God's gracious love and the restful well-being it brings are offered to

---

[22] G5485, *charis* (χάρις): grace, favor, kindness. It refers to goodwill that is freely given. Paul uses this word to emphasize God's unearned, overflowing generosity toward us in Christ.

[23] G1515, *eirēnē* (εἰρήνη): peace, wholeness, or wellbeing. It refers to more than the absence of conflict. In the Septuagint, it renders the Hebrew *shalom*, carrying the sense of flourishing life under God's blessing.

[24] Robert G. Bratcher and Eugene A. Nida, *A Handbook on Paul's Letter to the Ephesians*, UBS Handbook Series (New York: United Bible Societies, 1993), 5.

each of us in Christ. Grace and peace aren't just future promises. God wants to get them inside us now.

These two words pack a punch. William Barclay said that the mere mention of the word "grace" conjures thoughts of the sheer beauty of the Christian life and the unearned generosity of God's heart; true peace is found not through avoiding problems, but in doing God's will.[25] This beautiful grace and its accompanying peace are ours for the taking through Jesus.

When grace enters a conversation, shame must leave. When peace enters a church, bitterness loses its grip. Grace isn't just God's patience; it's God's empowering presence. And peace isn't passive; it's God's active wholeness, making broken people and broken communities well again. What would it look like if your church became known, above all else, for its grace and peace?

Paul writes all this to "you."[26] In Greek, this is the plural form of the second-person pronoun. Unfortunately, English doesn't distinguish between singular and plural "you," which can cause us to miss the communal tone of Paul's words. When someone says, "Hey, you!" we naturally assume that person

---

[25] William Barclay, *The Letters to the Galatians and Ephesians*, The New Daily Study Bible, 3rd ed (Louisville, KY: Westminster John Knox Press, 2002), 86–87.

[26] G5213, *hymin* (ὑμῖν): to you, for you (second person plural, dative). When Paul addresses "you" in Ephesians, he's communicating with the group.

means us as individuals. If I carry that assumption into this text, I might read Paul's blessing as a private message, just between God and me.

But Paul isn't speaking to one person in isolation. He's writing to a gathered group of people. His use of "you" is what we might call "y'all" in Texas. If you're from up north, maybe just imagine a holy version of "you all." Either way, Paul's greeting is not aimed at a solo believer but at the entire body of Christ.

God's grace and peace are for you and for the person sitting beside you. When Paul says "you" throughout this letter, he's addressing the whole community of saints. The theology in the first half of Ephesians and the practical instructions in the second are both meant to shape a people, not just a person.

In fact, *Getting the Church Inside Y'all* might be a better title for this book. We don't grow in grace alone. We can't experience lasting, divine peace apart from community. Contrary to the popular individualism that saturates modern faith, life in Christ is meant to be shared. The New Testament knows nothing of isolated discipleship. The grace and peace Paul offers are gifts meant to be received and lived together.

Imagine this letter being read aloud in a house church in Laodicea or among new believers in the bustling port city of Ephesus. Some had lost jobs because of their faith. Others faced pressure to conform to the culture around them. Most were still learning how to follow Jesus faithfully. And then they hear these words: "Grace to you and peace." As these words enter their ears and hearts, they don't hear critique or correction; they hear a message of blessing and belonging, a reminder of their identity in Christ.

Grace and peace from God our Father and the Lord Jesus Christ are exactly what we need. In a fractured world, Paul invites us to receive grace and extend it to others. In an anxious age, he offers peace, not as an escape, but as a grounding presence that anchors us in God's service.

To the child struggling to belong, the parent overwhelmed by fear, and the grandparent questioning his or her purpose, Paul begins with hope: "Grace to you and peace from God our Father and the Lord Jesus Christ." How do we press on in faith amid life's trials? How do we stay faithful when the pressure builds? How do we live with the church inside us?

Paul starts by naming us saints and blessing us with grace and peace. That feels like a good place for us to begin.

Praying the Message:

Lord Jesus, help us believe what You say about us. Help us receive the grace You give and walk in the peace You promise. Make us a church full of saints, not because we've earned the title, but because You've named us. Amen.

Further Reflection

Ephesians 1:1-2

1. **Context Connection**
   Paul opens his letter with a familiar greeting, yet Ephesians feels broader and more universal than some of his other writings.

   - What purpose might a "shared sermon" like this have served in the churches of Asia Minor during Paul's imprisonment?
   - How does thinking of Ephesians as a "circular letter," meant to be read by multiple congregations, help us hear it as a message for our communities today?

2. **Key Themes in the Text**
   Paul uses the word *saint* to describe not spiritual superstars, but ordinary believers made holy by God's grace.

   - How does this definition differ from the way the word is often used in our culture?
   - What difference might it make if we truly believed that *we*, and others in our church, are saints?

3. **Church and Community Application**
   Peterson acknowledges the critiques people raise about the church but presses a deeper question:

Do you actually worship with a congregation, share in its burdens, care for its children, walk with it through crises, and remain when relationships get messy?

Jesus honored the synagogue, formed a new community, and lived within the people of God, even when they turned against Him.[27]

- What strikes you about Peterson's reply?
- How might embracing Paul's vision of the church as a community of saints change how we view our church and ourselves?

4. **Personal Transformation**

   Paul begins this letter by offering grace and peace to the saints in Christ Jesus. Grace speaks of God's unearned favor. Peace (*eirēnē,* synonymous with *shalom*) points to God's wholeness and wellbeing that transcends circumstance.

   - What difference can this grace and peace make in your life today?
   - What difference might grace and peace make in our world?

5. **Closing Blessing or Prayer Prompt**
   May God bless you as you live in the grace and peace He offers freely through Christ Jesus our Lord.

[27] Peterson, *Practice Resurrection*, Kindle Page 934–36.

Chapter 2

A Prayerful Reminder of the Larger Story Ephesians 1:3–23

Blessed be the God and Father of our Lord Jesus Christ, who has blessed us in Christ with every spiritual blessing in the heavenly places, even as he chose us in him before the foundation of the world, that we should be holy and blameless before him. In love he predestined us for adoption to himself as sons through Jesus Christ, according to the purpose of his will, to the praise of his glorious grace, with which he has blessed us in the Beloved.
(Ephesians 1:3-6)

Picture this: a young couple in the morning rush: work prep, lunchboxes, backpacks, coffee still too hot to sip. Their youngest sounds gravelly. "Allergy meds," Mom says, heading for the kitchen. Dad nods and hustles her into the car for the school drop-off on the way to his big meeting. Twenty minutes later, the nurse calls: "Pick her up. Doctor's note required."

One parent misses work. The child misses instruction time. The doctor confirms the obvious (seasonal allergies), writes the note, and the child is back at school. After all that, the day ends where it began—at home.

It is more than an inconvenience. It is the stuck-in-a-loop feeling you cannot shake. Zoom out and you see more: post-pandemic rules, social fatigue, and community anxiety.

Most of life unfolds in a frame we cannot see in the moment. That is true for small hassles and soul-deep aches: canceled flights, failed interviews, or loneliness on a Sunday. They weigh more when we realize they are part of something larger.

We are meaning-hungry people. From childhood, we search for a story to inhabit. That is why kids beg, "Read it again!" after bedtime. It is not just fun; it is how we make sense of the world. When trouble comes, our first question is often, "Why?" We do not just ask for an answer but to find our place in the plot.

Miss God's story, and you will be swept into lesser ones: performance, popularity, pressure, or pain.

Paul will not let the Ephesians or us start there. Before he gives commands, he writes a song. Not "behave" or "fix this," but a sweeping vision of who God is and what He has done. One long sentence in Greek, 202 words of breathless praise, rises like a tide and pulls our tangled stories into the vast ocean of God's eternal plan.

This praise reminds us that however messy our chapter feels, our story is anchored in God's purposes. This is exactly what Paul's vision invites us to do: take the fragments of our daily lives and place them in the context of God's eternal story.

Spiritual Practice: Story Reframing

Take five minutes today to name one part of your story that feels unfinished or small. Write it in a single sentence:

- "I feel stuck at work."
- "I'm grieving a relationship I can't fix."
- "I don't know where God is leading me."

Now, read Ephesians 1:3–14 aloud. Ask God to help you see that part of your life inside His larger story of grace, adoption, redemption, and promise. Rewrite your sentence as a declaration of truth:

- "Even though I feel stuck at work, I am still chosen, redeemed, and marked as God's own."
- "Even though my relationship is broken, I am loved by God."
- "I'm not sure where God is leading me, but I believe He is leading me."

Keep this new sentence with you this week as a phone note, bookmark, or sticky note on your mirror. Let it remind you that your story belongs to God, and He is still writing it.

Paul takes this same practice and stretches it across eternity, showing us who we are in Christ no matter our circumstance.

Praise That Reframes Our Perspective

Paul's prayer in Ephesians meets our deep hunger for meaning. His song begins "before the foundation of the world" and stretches into eternity. It's as if he takes our cluttered timeline of deadlines, disappointments, and detours and lays it over God's eternal calendar. Suddenly, our moments are measured against forever.

This is not a pep talk to boost morale or a positive-thinking exercise to "look on the bright side." It is a theological declaration: God's purposes are older than the sun and more certain than tomorrow's sunrise. They were set in motion before the first bird sang or the first wave touched the shore.

Our culture offers different scripts:

- You are what you achieve.
- You are what others think of you.
- You are how you feel today.

Each is exhausting because the story changes as soon as we fail, fall out of favor, or wake up in a bad mood. Paul offers a better identity:

- You are who God says you are,
- because of what Christ has done,
- and because the Spirit lives in you.

This identity does not crumble when your emotions shift or your reputation suffers.

Paul writes this from prison. The chains on his wrists are real, the stone walls around him cold. Yet his words are soaked in joy. His heart is not chained to the cell; it is anchored in the throne room of God.

From the outside, Paul's situation looked hopeless: stripped of freedom, awaiting trial, with no promise of release. From the inside, through the lens of praise, Paul saw heaven's horizon. His words read like those of a man on tiptoe, catching sight of a reality that dwarfs the iron bars in front of him.

Paul's perspective is not denial. It is defiance. It's the choice to say, "My present circumstances do not get the final word." Praise reframes our perspective so that God's unshakable kingdom becomes clearer than the shifting shadows of our troubles.

Paul was not the last to write with hope in hardship. Over 1800 years later, Charlotte "Lottie" Moon left the comfort of Virginia to serve in northern China. Conditions were not just inconvenient; they were dangerous. She learned the language, lived among the people, taught in schools, endured civil unrest, deep loneliness, harsh winters, and repeated famines. Often, she went hungry so the children in her care could eat, giving away her own food until she weighed less than fifty pounds.

Her letters did not sugarcoat the suffering. She wrote honestly of spiritual darkness and physical need, yet, like Paul, anchored her hope in eternity: "Surely there can be no greater joy than that of saving souls." Even as her body weakened, her vision of God's kingdom burned brighter. When she died on Christmas Eve 1912 aboard a ship bound for home, her earthly mission was unfinished, but her eternal influence continues.[28]

Like Paul, Lottie could have let hardship justify her retreat. Instead, she looked at life through the horizon of heaven. Her praise was not the denial of hardship; it was defiance against despair.

Paul's invitation to the Ephesians is the same for us: Root your identity in the unshakable truth of who you are in Christ, chosen and adopted into God's family.

Behind Paul's unshakable joy is an unshakable truth. Before the first sunrise, God had already chosen him and welcomed him into His family. That same truth is yours in Christ.

---

[28] Lottie Moon, *Send the Light: Lottie Moon's Letters and Other Writings*, ed. Keith Harper (Macon, GA: Mercer University Press, 2002), 368; Catherine B. Allen, *The New Lottie Moon Story* (Nashville, TN: Broadman Press, 1980), 267.

Chosen and Adopted by the Father

Paul begins with identity: "Blessed be the God and Father… who has blessed us… just as He chose us in Him before the foundation of the world."[29]

Words like *chosen, adopted, redeemed,* and *sealed* are not abstract theological concepts floating in the clouds. They are the vocabulary of family. They speak of belonging, homecoming, and the security of knowing your name is written into God's own family history.

To be *chosen* in Paul's world meant more than being picked for a team. It meant being singled out with intention and purpose. In Israel's story, God chose Abraham, not because he was the most powerful or influential, but because God delighted to work through him. He chose Israel, calling the nation His "firstborn son" (Exod. 4:22), not because they were more numerous or impressive than other nations, but simply because He loved them and was keeping His promises (Deut. 7:7–8). Through the prophet Hosea, God promised, *"I will call those who were not my people, 'My people'"* (Rom. 9:25, quoting a Greek version of Hosea 2:23).

Paul takes that same covenant language and applies it to every believer, Jew and Gentile alike. God's choice

---

[29] G1586, *eklegomai,* (ἐξελέξατο): to choose, pick out, or select from among others. It carries the nuance of intentionality; God's choice is deliberate and purposeful, rooted in love, not chance (Eph. 1:4).

of you was never reluctant, never random, and never based on merit. It was rooted in His loving plan.

I think of dear friends of ours, both white, who adopted an African American son. At first, their differences were obvious. But as the years passed, something beautiful unfolded. The boy laughed like his father. He used turns of phrase he'd learned from his mother. Sometimes, I honestly forgot he was adopted. What made them family wasn't biology; it was love, belonging, and a shared life.

Paul's readers in Ephesus would have felt the weight of these words. In Roman law, adoption was never casual.[30] It was a formal, binding legal act, often undertaken by wealthy or influential families to secure an heir. The moment of adoption legally transferred a person from one family into another. Every debt from that person's old life was erased. Adopted children gained full legal standing and, in some ways, even greater security than natural-born children. As Bible teacher Eddie Rasnake notes, a Roman father could disown a natural-born child, but an adopted child could not be disowned. Roman law made adoption irrevocable.[31]

---

[30] G5206, *huiothesia* (υἱοθεσία): adoption. It comes from two Greek words meaning to place or set as a son. It refers to the legal act of formally establishing someone as a son or daughter with full inheritance rights (Eph. 1:5).

[31] Eddie Rasnake, *The Book of Ephesians*, Following God Through the Bible (Chattanooga, TN: AMG Publishers, 2003), 19.

This is more than a legal transaction; it's a turning of the page in the greatest story ever told. Adoption means our story is no longer random or uncertain; it has been written into God's own family history.

That's why Paul's statement would have stunned his audience. Many of the Ephesian believers were Gentiles, outsiders to the covenant God had made with Israel. They had been strangers to God's promises. Yet Paul looks them in the eye and says, in effect: "You've been chosen and legally transferred into God's household, with your debts erased, full rights as heirs, and an adoption that can never be undone."

Saved and Redeemed by the Son

Paul doesn't stop with the beautiful language of adoption; he adds another word rich with meaning: *redeemed.*

In the ancient world, redemption was the act of paying the price to liberate a slave from bondage.[32] It was freedom bought at a cost, sometimes by a generous benefactor, sometimes by a family member. For the Ephesians, who lived in a society built on patronage, debt, and transactional relationships, this was revolutionary. God wasn't negotiating for their loyalty or bargaining for their favor. He had already paid the full price for their freedom in Christ.

---

[32] G629, *apolutrōsis* (ἀπολύτρωσις): redemption or release by paying a ransom. The term often referred to freeing slaves, but Paul uses it here to describe spiritual liberation purchased by Christ's blood (Eph. 1:7).

I think of those same friends who adopted their son. Every year they celebrate his "Gotcha Day," the anniversary of when his adoption became official. They'd share his favorite meal, retell the story, and give thanks for the joy of being family. It reminds me of what I often tell my own kids: "If someone lined up all the children your age in the whole world, I'd choose you every time." That's the heart of the Father toward His children, and that is the very spirit of God's redemption.

In a world obsessed with measuring people by performance, beauty, or usefulness, God's adoption and redemption speak a different word. We are not "just enough." We are wanted. We are loved. We are brought home. And when God adopts us, He begins to reshape us. We start to resemble our adoptive family. We speak the language of grace. We bear the fruit of the Spirit. Our old identity isn't erased; it's redeemed.

That's what Jesus did for us. He entered our chains, bore our shame, and paid the price Himself. His grace wasn't rationed like a miser counting coins. It was lavished.[33]

I once caught a glimpse of that kind of grace when my old truck broke down in a small Texas town. It was the middle of summer, and the heat shimmered off the asphalt like waves. I had just enough money for a

---

[33] G4052, *perisseuō* (περισσεύω): to abound, overflow, be in excess; to cause to abound, to lavish upon. This refers to the superabundant measure of God's grace (Eph. 1:8).

questionable motel room and a couple of sandwiches from a restaurant down the street to sustain my hungry, teenage brother-in-law and me. Unsure what to do, I called my dad. Without hesitation, he dropped what he was doing, drove hours across the state, paid for the repairs, and got us home.

There was no lecture about maintenance nor any judgment about planning ahead. Instead, my dad offered his steady presence and provision. That's how Jesus rescues, but on an eternal scale: by meeting us in our stranded, overheated, and helpless places and getting us home.

I also think of a young mother addicted to heroin who once sank into my office couch as if it were the last safe place in the world. With hollow eyes and a trembling voice, she said, "Things are so bad that my skin hurts pressed against this couch." She wasn't speaking in metaphor. Her entire body ached under the weight of her choices, her withdrawal symptoms, and her shame.

Years later, after she and her family endured a hard uphill struggle toward sobriety by leaning into their faith in Jesus, her posture had changed. The eyes that once revealed agony and shame now glimmered with new life. With fire in her voice, she said, "Jesus saved my life." That's redemption. It's not just forgiveness for the past but the restoration of someone who had been all but lost—a life rebuilt on grace as its foundation.

Redemption is God taking our broken plotlines and weaving them into His unshakable story of grace, where even the most painful chapters become part of His glory.

In the ancient world, a redeemed slave was often given a new name, new clothes, and a place at the table. So it is with us. We are forgiven by grace, renamed in love, and seated with Christ.

Chosen, adopted, redeemed, and seated with Him: this is who we are in God's story, a story that began before the foundation of the world and that will never end.

Sealed by the Spirit

We are not only adopted and redeemed; we are also marked as God's own. Paul says we are "sealed[34] with the promised Holy Spirit, who is the guarantee[35] of our inheritance" (Ephesians 1:13–14 ESV). This seal is God's way of permanently inscribing your life into His story, a mark that your place in His kingdom is secure and your future is already woven into His plan.

In the ancient world, a seal signified ownership, authenticity, and protection. Archaeological discoveries

---

[34] G4972, *sphragizō* (σφραγίζω): to seal or to mark for security, ownership, or authenticity. The Spirit's seal marks believers as God's own (Eph. 1:13).

[35] G728, *arrabōn* (ἀρραβών): "guarantee." A commercial term meaning "down payment, earnest money," a pledge guaranteeing full future payment. In Paul's writing, the Spirit is the foretaste of our full inheritance (Eph. 1:14).

and ancient texts describe how engraved signet rings or cylindrical seals were pressed into clay or wax to leave a distinct impression that identified a sender or owner. A king's seal on a document or decree declared, "This is mine. It bears my authority." Legal contracts, letters, and cargo shipments were sealed to guarantee their origin and protect them from tampering. Merchants sealed their goods before transport, and soldiers sometimes carried sealed orders that could not be opened until the appointed time. Breaking a seal without permission carried serious consequences.[36]

Scholars note that Paul's use of the verb "to seal" evokes this imagery of ownership and security. As one study explains, in the Greco-Roman world, "the metaphor of sealing expressed belonging, authenticity, and protection under one's authority."[37] A seal proved that what was marked belonged to someone of higher standing and was safeguarded by that person's power.

---

[36] Archaeological and biblical evidence shows that seals in the ancient world signified ownership, authenticity, and protection. See Othmar Keel, *The Symbolism of the Biblical World: Ancient Near Eastern Iconography and the Book of Psalms*, trans. Timothy J. Hallett (Winona Lake, IN: Eisenbrauns, 1997), 248–50; and Clinton E. Arnold, *Ephesians*, Zondervan Exegetical Commentary on the New Testament (Grand Rapids, MI: Zondervan, 2010), 109-110.

[37] Arnold, *Ephesians*, 109–111; see also F. F. Bruce, *The Epistles to the Colossians, to Philemon, and to the Ephesians*, The New International Commentary on the New Testament (Grand Rapids, MI: Eerdmans, 1984), 266–67; Lynn Cohick, *Ephesians: A New Covenant Commentary* (Eugene, OR: Cascade Books, 2020), 43.

Similarly, Paul's imagery tells believers that God Himself has claimed them as His own and has placed His Spirit within them as both proof and promise.

God has done the same with you, not with wax or ink, but with His own Spirit. The seal is not merely a mark placed on you but the very presence of God living in you, testifying that you belong to Him, that your faith is genuine, and that your inheritance is secure. The Spirit is not a temporary stamp but the living pledge that the full weight of God's promises will one day be delivered in person.

When Lisa's mother, Judith, died suddenly in a car accident, the news hit like a blow we couldn't absorb. The days that followed were a blur of funeral arrangements, phone calls, and quiet tears that came without warning. In the middle of that fog, an envelope arrived in the mail. Inside was a note from one of Judith's coworkers, a woman we'd only met briefly in a passing exchange at a memorial service.

She wrote of her deep admiration and respect for Judith. In just a short time, Lisa's mom had made a profound impact on her new coworkers through her kindness and joy-filled spirit. This woman shared small but vivid stories of how Judith lit up when she spoke about her children and her first grandchild and how her eyes sparkled with tenderness when she mentioned her family.

She described specific details about what was going on in each of our lives and how proud we made Judith.

The only way she could have known those things in the short time she knew Judith was if Judith talked about us all the time.

Reading those words felt like opening a treasure chest of memories we hadn't lived but now got to share. It was the most valuable kind of inheritance, not money or possessions but the deep assurance that we were loved and spoken well of, even when we weren't in the room. It was a gift to be reminded that we were treasured deeply by someone who meant so much to all of us.

That letter became, in its own way, a seal of remembrance. It testified that Judith's love was still at work, her story still marking the lives of those she touched. In a far greater way, the Holy Spirit does the same for us. He bears witness that we belong to God and that His love continues to shape our story, even when life feels fragile or unfinished.

That is what the Spirit does. He brings the Father's voice to our hearts, reminds us we belong, and gives us a foretaste of the joy that's coming. He is not just the echo of a promise. He is our *guarantee*, a divine down payment on the glory to come.[38] The Holy Spirit's presence assures us that we are indeed heirs of every blessing secured in Christ.

It's as if God placed a banner over your life that reads: *Signed by grace. Marked by My presence. Reserved for*

---

38 Hoehner, "Ephesians," 619.

eternity. Because these blessings are already ours, Paul does the most pastoral thing he can do. He prays that we would see them clearly and live based on them.

Paul's Prayer for the Church

After declaring these blessings, Paul turns from praise to prayer. He asks that *the eyes of our hearts* would be enlightened, that we would not just hear these truths, but see them, trust them, and live based on them. He longs for believers to grasp

- **The hope of God's calling**: the steady anchor of knowing we have been summoned into His story, chosen with purpose, and promised a future that cannot be stolen.
- **The riches of His glorious inheritance in His people**: the breathtaking reality that God treasures His church and delights to dwell among His redeemed.
- **The immeasurable greatness of His power toward us who believe**: a power without limit and without expiration.

That power, Paul says, is *resurrection power*. It is the same power that broke the grip of the grave and seated Jesus above every authority, every ruler, and every name that will ever be spoken. No system, no force of darkness, and no cultural tide can rival His reign. And because your King is alive, your future is secure.

I see this resurrection power at work as I walk with people through life. A married couple engaging each other with tender gentleness where there had once been bitter turmoil—that is resurrection power. A once-troubled child who begins to find his or her way—that is resurrection power. A person who once lacked confidence passing an important test and receiving a promotion—this, too, is resurrection power. When lives are transformed, God's power is on display. The same Spirit who rolled away the stone is still raising the fallen and breathing life into what once seemed beyond hope.

When Paul says Christ is *"head over all things to the church,"* he reminds us that the One who fills the universe also fills His people. We are His body, animated by His Spirit, carrying His presence into classrooms, boardrooms, living rooms, and hospital rooms. The fullness of Christ is not confined to heaven; He lives and moves through His people, filling the world with His presence until the day we see Him face to face.

We are loved by the Father, freed by the Son, and kept by the Spirit. In that promise, Paul's prayer becomes ours.

Praying the Message

Father of grace, thank You for writing us into Your story of love and belonging. You chose, adopted, and welcomed us, not because we earned it but because You delighted to call us Your children. Thank You for Jesus, who redeemed us with His blood, and for the

Spirit, Who seals us and reminds us of our place in Your family.

When we feel lost, remind us of our hope. When we feel weak, remind us of the power that raised Christ from the dead and now lives in us. Open our eyes to the hope we have, the inheritance we share, and the grace we carry. Let our lives reflect the joy of being redeemed, sealed, and deeply loved. Lift our eyes beyond the detours of our days and place our small stories inside the beauty of Your great story. Amen.

Further Reflection

Ephesians 1:3-23

1. **Context Connection**
   N.T. Wright describes this passage as "a celebration of the larger story within which every single Christian story—every story of individual conversion, faith, spiritual life, obedience and hope—is set."[39] We all carry personal stories, some joyful, some painful. Paul's prayer invites us to place those stories within the larger story of God's redeeming love.

   - Where are you in your story right now?
   - What challenges or joys are shaping your days? How might God be at work in the middle of them?

[39] Wright, *Paul for Everyone*, 8.

2. **Key Themes in the Text**
   We are "chosen" by the Father and "adopted" into His family. We have "redemption through His blood" and are "sealed" with the Holy Spirit as the guarantee of our inheritance.

   - What does it mean to you to be chosen and adopted by God? How does this reshape your view of your worth, your past, or your place in the church?
   - How do you understand the work Jesus did to deliver us from sin? How does this connect to your identity as a child of God?
   - Have you ever made or received a down payment? How might the Spirit's presence help you trust God's promises more fully?

3. **Church and Community Application**
   Paul's vision in this passage is not just individual but communal; God's larger story is unfolding through His people together.

   - How can your church help its members see their personal stories as part of God's bigger redemptive story?
   - How might we better remind each other that we are chosen, redeemed, and sealed?

4. **Personal Transformation**

   Paul ends this section by praying for believers to know the hope, riches, and power they have in Christ.

   - Read verses 15-23 slowly. How would you rewrite this prayer in your own words for your life right now?
   - What might change in your daily outlook if you truly believed you are empowered by the same power that raised Christ from the dead?

5. **Closing Blessing or Prayer Prompt**
   Lord, anchor my small story in Your great story. Remind me daily that I am chosen, redeemed, sealed, and empowered to live for Your glory. Amen.

CHAPTER 3

FROM DEATH TO LIFE: A TALE OF TWO FUNERALS EPHESIANS 2

For by grace you have been saved through faith. And this is not your own doing; it is the gift of God, not a result of works, so that no one may boast. For we are his workmanship, created in Christ Jesus for good works, which God prepared beforehand, that we should walk in them.

(Ephesians 2:8-10)

The sanctuary was full that afternoon. Sunlight streamed through the stained-glass windows, casting colored patterns across the casket at the front. Family members sat shoulder to shoulder, holding hands, tears mixing with quiet smiles as stories of faith and kindness filled the room. The woman we honored had a way of leaving every place better with her steady smile, warm laughter, and generous spirit. She had lived her faith out loud to the end.

I stood at the pulpit with Paul's words from 1 Corinthians 15 open before me, words I've read more times than I can count: *"Death is swallowed up in victory. O death, where is your victory? O death, where is your sting?"* Her life and faith made those words easy to proclaim. Here was a saint of God whose joy pointed us to Jesus and whose death was precious in the sight of the Lord.

Not long afterward, I stood in the same sanctuary. This time, the crowd was smaller and quieter. The woman we remembered had also followed Christ, but her life had been marked more by struggle than ease. Her loved ones described her as stern, serious, and often lonely. Her faith was real, but the wounds of a hard life had left scars that never fully healed this side of eternity.

As I prepared her service, I found myself asking, What can I say here? That's when Paul's words to the Ephesians came to mind: *"But God, being rich in mercy… made us alive together with Christ—by grace you have been saved."* The same grace that claimed the first woman had claimed the second. One bore the fruit of grace in joy and warmth. The other bore the marks of grace in endurance and faith through hardship. These women had different personalities and stories but embraced the same gospel and found the same victory over death.

But God…

Paul's "But God" in Ephesians 2 is not just a theological transition. It is a rescue signal flaring across the night sky. It is the sound of shackles hitting the floor. It is the first gasp of breath after you've been pulled from deep water.

Before it, Paul paints our condition with honesty: we were dead in sin,[40] enslaved, and without hope. No amount of self-help or moral reform could change our lost, spiritually dead condition.

Then come the two words that change everything: But God.

We were sinking, but God dove in. We were enemies, but God made peace. We were far off, but God brought us near. This is the divine interruption, the moment the Author writes Himself into the story.

"Being rich in mercy…because of the great love with which he loved us… even when we were dead in our trespasses." Paul makes it clear that salvation begins and ends with God's initiative. The funerals of those two women reminded me that salvation is never about merit or personality. It is about the dead who are made alive in Christ.

And once God calls you to life, everything changes. You are raised with Christ, seated with Him, and swept into the immeasurable riches of His grace. You are His workmanship, crafted for a life you could not have imagined before He found you.

---

40 G3498, *nekros* (νεκρός): "dead," "corpse." Used here to establish Paul's spiritual diagnosis: lifeless, powerless, incapable of self-revival.

This is the gospel Paul celebrates in Ephesians 2. It's good news that saves us for eternity and transforms us in the present. It raises the dead, reconciles enemies, and breaks down the walls we build between each other.

John Stott reminds us: "We must never think of salvation as a human achievement. It is a divine work from beginning to end."[41] God does not meet us halfway. He comes all the way into our grave and raises us. He initiates, sustains, and completes the miracle.

From Death to Life in Real Time

I have stood at the bedside of the dying. I have watched doctors call the time of death. I have read Scripture and prayed with people as they closed their eyes in this world and opened them in the next. I have seen families weep under the weight of finality. In those moments, no one imagines the person can rescue themselves. That is why Paul's next words in Ephesians 2 are so powerful. Only God can bring the dead to life. Only God can reach into the flatlined reality of our sin and restart the heart.

Paul describes the same kind of moment we see in John 11, when Jesus stands at the tomb of Lazarus. He had been dead for four days and was beyond hope. Yet with a word, Jesus calls him forth. Lazarus did not unbind himself. He did not stagger out on his own

---

[41] John Stott, *The Message of Romans: God's Good News for the World* (Downers Grove, IL: InterVarsity Press, 1994), 107.

initiative. He came because the voice of the Son of God reached into death and called him to life.

N.T. Wright reminds us, "The resurrection completes the inauguration of God's kingdom… It is not an escape from the world, but the rescue of the world."[42] The new life God gives is not only a promise of heaven but also the beginning of His restoration project right here, right now.

This is what grace looks like in its rawest form—resurrection power offered to people who can do nothing to earn it. In a world that applauds effort and achievement, the gospel reminds us that our only boast is in the mercy of God who makes the dead live again.

We cannot make light of the wages of our sin. We were not simply misdirected or immature. We were spiritually dead. We followed the world's path, obeyed the voice of darkness, and were shaped by disobedience. This spiritual death was not abstract. It was active. We walked in sin. We followed brokenness. We gave in to the desires of the flesh. Paul includes himself and all believers in this indictment: "Among whom we all once lived... and were by nature children of wrath" (Eph. 2:3 ESV).

Verse 4 brings the pivot: "But God." With those two words, despair turns to hope, death to life. "But God, being rich in mercy, because of the great love with

---

[42] N.T. Wright, *Surprised by Hope: Rethinking Heaven, the Resurrection, and the Mission of the Church* (New York: HarperOne, 2008), 218.

which he loved us... made us alive together with Christ" (Eph. 2:4–5 ESV). In Christ, God did what we could not do for ourselves. He breathed life into our spiritually dead condition. We are not rescued because of our goodness. We are raised because of God's mercy.

A Resurrection Story Up Close

Early one evening, in an earlier ministry context, I received a call from a family who had been visiting our church. They had questions and wondered if I could come by. My calendar was clear, a rare gift in pastoral life, so within the hour I was in their apartment, listening to their story.

The husband, recently released from prison, said he was considering baptism but didn't want it to be just a "jailhouse conversion." He wanted to be sure his faith was real.

Then his wife took a deep breath, bracing herself to share something heavy. Her voice trembled. "When he first started serving his sentence, I found out I was pregnant," she said. "I could not imagine raising our baby alone. I did not know how to make ends meet. And I was terrified. So... I had an abortion."

She looked away, wiping a tear. "I never thought I would feel so terrible about it," she continued. "I pray every night for forgiveness, but I just cannot seem to find peace. I have asked God so many times, but I do not know if He hears me. I just wish I had a sign that I have been forgiven. If God could give me a sign of His forgiveness, I could move on."

I paused, letting her words settle. "It is no accident that I answered your call today," I said. "My family was out of town, and my schedule was open. I believe God allowed me to be here right now so I could say this to you: God loves you. In Christ, your sins are forgiven."

As the truth sank in, something shifted. Her shoulders relaxed. Tears filled her eyes, but they were not just tears of sorrow. They were tears of release. Heaven's grace broke through her shame and grief in an almost tangible way, and she dared to believe forgiveness could be hers.

She was baptized the next Sunday, and months later her husband followed.

In the years since, God has blessed them with steady work, faithful friends, and new babies to love. Today they serve the Lord faithfully and continue to grow in Christ as a family. What the world might have written off, grace redeemed. Only God can do that.

This is exactly Who Paul describes in Ephesians 2: the God who finds us in the graveyard of our sins and calls us to life in Christ. This couple's story is a living picture of what it means to be raised with Him, seated with Him, and remade for His purposes.

God's Handiwork

Paul does not stop at personal salvation. No longer dead in sin, believers can live differently because they are united with Christ in His resurrected life. In Christ, God's new creation has begun, and our lives should reflect that reality. Because we have been delivered from sin and death, we can now pursue lives that bring joy to God's heart.

Paul is emphatic: "For by grace you have been saved through faith. And this is not your own doing; it is the gift of God, not a result of works, so that no one may boast" (Eph. 2:8–9 ESV). Salvation is not a reward for good behavior but the gracious gift of a loving God.

Paul continues, "We are his workmanship,[43] created in Christ Jesus for good works, which God prepared beforehand, that we should walk in them" (Eph. 2:10 ESV). Wright notes that this Greek word for *workmanship* often carries an artistic meaning, describing a sculpture, song, painting, or poem: a masterpiece. We are God's creative project, a living work through which He displays His glory. Paul's image is like a musical score: notes on a page that come alive when played. In Christ, we are given back the music of a fully human life designed by God and filled with purpose.[44]

Paul grounds that image in everyday life. We are not saved by good works but saved for them. Grace

---

[43] G4161, *poiēma* (ποίημα): workmanship, that which is made, creation, masterpiece. Used only here and in Romans 1:20, where it refers to God's creation in nature; in this verse *poiēma* describes believers as God's intentional handiwork, created in Christ Jesus for good works.

[44] Wright, *Paul for Everyone*, 24.

redeems us from sin and reclaims us for a purpose. These works show up in classrooms, repair shops, homes, and neighborhoods—wherever Spirit-enabled love is lived out.

What about you? What good works has God prepared for you? What passions, skills, or resources has He entrusted to you for His kingdom? Whom has He placed around you to love and serve? These are holy questions worth prayerful attention.

You are God's workmanship, not a random collection of parts but a handcrafted creation, uniquely gifted and intentionally placed. When we live out our callings with humility and joy, we become living testimonies of God's grace in action. Paul's vision of grace moves beyond individual lives to form something new: a reconciled community.

Spiritual Practice: Walk the Grace Line

At the start of each day this week, reflect on this simple phrase from Ephesians 2: "But God…" Write those words at the top of a journal page or in a note on your phone. Then complete the sentence for yourself, naming how God has met you in your past and how He might want to move in your present.

- *"I was stuck in shame, but God reminded me I am forgiven."*
- *"I was afraid to reach out, but God gave me courage."*
- *"I was walking in pride, but God humbled me with love."*

- At the end of each day, pause and ask yourself:
- How did grace show up today?
- Where did I see God bringing life where there once was death?

This is more than reflection; it is resurrection recognition. When we name the "But God" moments in our stories, we become more aware of how grace is shaping our walks, step-by-step, day by day, for the good works God has prepared for us.

A New Community

God's great handiwork is reflected in the new kind of family being formed with Jesus as its foundation.[45] God is working to bring unity and oneness where there has been division and discord. No longer divided into camps like Jew and Gentile, we are being united in Christ. In a world fractured by politics, race, ethnicity, and culture, God is building one new people. We are fellow citizens, saints, and members of God's household (2:19).

With Christ as our cornerstone, we are being built into a holy temple where God dwells by His Spirit (2:20–22). Paul's vision of unity was not theoretical; it was radical, practical, and deeply needed in both his day and ours.

---

[45] David S. Dockery, "The Pauline Letters," in *Holman Concise Bible Commentary*, ed. David S. Dockery (Nashville, TN: Broadman & Holman Publishers, 1998), 577.

Paul does not only celebrate individual salvation; he proclaims the creation of an entirely new community. Beginning in verse 11, Paul shifts from personal resurrection to corporate reconciliation. He reminds Gentile believers that they were once outsiders "separated from Christ, alienated from the commonwealth of Israel, and strangers to the covenants of promise" (v. 12). They had no hope and were without God. But now, because of the blood of Christ, they have been brought near, not only to God, but to one another.

The significance of that statement in Paul's world cannot be overstated. The division between Jews and Gentiles was deep, painful, and entrenched. It was not merely theological; it was ethnic, cultural, and social. Jews often saw Gentiles as unclean, lawless, and idolatrous. Gentiles viewed Jews as strange, judgmental, and exclusive.

In the Jerusalem temple, a literal wall separated the Court of the Gentiles from the inner courts reserved for Jews. Archaeologists have discovered inscriptions warning Gentiles not to enter: "No foreigner may enter within the barrier…" Paul likely had this in mind when he wrote, "*Christ… has broken down the dividing wall of hostility*" (v. 14). In one powerful image, he declares that through the cross, Jesus demolished not just stone barriers but the hostility and exclusion they represented.

We need this word today. Our world is fractured by divisions of race, politics, generations, denominations, and more. We categorize, stereotype, and cancel. Even the church, which should model a better way, often mirrors the culture's fault lines. Paul reminds us that Christ came not only to forgive our sins but to forge a new kind of family.

What would it look like for the American church to live as one reconciled people? It would mean choosing humility over tribalism, listening instead of labeling, and building bridges instead of bunkers. It would mean letting our shared identity in Christ outweigh our differences in background, class, or culture. We would see one another not as threats or strangers, but as fellow citizens, saints, and members of God's household (v. 19).

At our church, we have two services in English and one in Spanish. Periodically, we worship together in both languages. It's clunky and beautiful. Monolingual folks can feel lost; bilinguals sometimes grow impatient. But we keep doing it because it pictures God's kingdom.

Ephesians 2 reminds us that reconciliation is not optional. It is the natural outflow of grace. Jesus did not die to make us polite strangers; He died to make us family. He is building a temple not with bricks and mortar but with people, making friends out of those who once were enemies. We were once separated by many barriers and conflicts. Now, because of Jesus, we are joined together in peace.

In a divided world, the church must embody the gospel of peace. Our unity does not erase our differences; it redeems them. When we live that unity, we become what Paul says we already are: a holy temple, where the God of resurrection still dwells.

True worship can happen in multiple languages, among different generations, and across socioeconomic divides because God's purpose is to renew creation and restore a broken world. We have grown too accustomed to the divisiveness that defines our cultural landscape. The gospel of grace that brings hope at a funeral also empowers us to build a new family in this broken world.

Hard seasons, filled with illness, loss, and death, remind us that life is short. They also remind us that life in Christ is everlasting. Through the saving power of Jesus, we participate in God's redemption story. Even when the world seems determined to find new ways to hate and harm, we cling to the truth: we are God's workmanship, and through us, He is creating something beautiful.

Some days that beauty shines clearly, like in the first funeral story. Other days, as in the second story, we may need to look more closely to see God's fingerprints. But it is His grace and handiwork that make all the difference. At the end of it all, after grace has saved, transformed, and united us, it leaves a mark.

God writes a melody in us. God puts His signature upon us. What we call a testimony, Paul calls God's good workmanship.

You are God's workmanship: handcrafted, uniquely placed, and redeemed to join God's kingdom work. Every act of faithfulness is a brushstroke on His masterpiece. Whether your life shines with joy or endures in struggle, God's grace leaves its mark.

Praying the Message

Lord of grace, thank You for saving us when we were dead in sin and for calling us into new life in Christ. Make us living signs of Your mercy. Help us to walk in the good works You have prepared and to tear down the walls that divide us. Shape us into a people who reflects Your love and let our lives sing the song of Your grace. In Jesus's name, Amen.

Further Reflection

Ephesians 2

1. **Context Connection**
   Paul's words in Ephesians 2 remind us that we were once dead in sin, but God, rich in mercy and love, made us alive with Christ. Salvation is not an achievement; it is a gift. This gift doesn't just change our eternity; it transforms our present.

   - What stood out to you in the two funeral stories? Have you experienced a moment that helped you better understand the depth of God's grace?

- According to Paul, what does it mean to be "dead in sin"? What does it mean to be "made alive in Christ"?

2. **Key Themes in the Text**
   We are God's workmanship, created in Christ Jesus for good works that He prepared in advance for us.

   - How does Ephesians 2 challenge the assumption that salvation is something we earn?
   - What does it mean to you that you are God's workmanship? How does that shape how you see yourself and others?
   - What good works might God be calling you to walk in right now? What gifts or opportunities has He placed in your hands?

3. **Church and Community Application**
   Christ has "broken down the dividing wall of hostility," creating one new humanity and reconciling us to God and each other.

   - What modern walls does the gospel invite us to confront and dismantle?
   - In a divided world, how can the church embody the unity and peace described in this chapter?

4. **Personal Transformation**
   Grace empowers us to live differently in every role we have: at home, at work, in our neighborhoods, and within the church.

   - How do you think grace empowers your everyday vocation as a parent, student, worker, neighbor, or friend?
   - How can you personally be a peacemaker in your church, community, or relationships?

5. **Closing Blessing or Prayer Prompt**
   Lord, thank You for making me alive in Christ. Teach me to walk in the good works You have prepared and to live as a peacemaker, reflecting Your grace and reconciliation in all I do. Amen.

Chapter 4

That's My Brother: A Barrier-Defying Gospel Ephesians 3

This mystery is that the Gentiles are fellow heirs, members of the same body, and partakers of the promise in Christ Jesus through the gospel.
(Ephesians 3:6)

Imagine receiving a letter in the mail from an attorney representing the family down the street. You do not know that family well. There have been a few tensions over the years, but you have always tried to be cordial. Curious and a little anxious, you open the envelope, bracing for bad news.

The first paragraph informs you that this family has just inherited a massive estate. You pause, thinking, "Well, good for them," but you still do not understand why their lawyer is writing to you. Then you read the next paragraph again to be sure you do not misunderstand. It says this family, now incredibly wealthy, has initiated a legal process to invite you into their clan and is offering you an equal share in their inheritance.

It is outrageous. Most of us would dismiss such a message as a scam. (A few of you may be tempted to check your mailboxes just in case.) We can hardly imagine receiving such extravagant news. Yet this is exactly the kind of shocking, too-good-to-be-true announcement Paul makes to the believers in and around Ephesus. This is the heart of the gospel.

Paul had been entrusted by God with a mystery hidden for generations but now revealed in Christ: the astonishing grace of God extends not only to Israel but to the Gentiles as well.[46] Those once considered outsiders are now full participants in the family of God. They are embraced as co-heirs with a seat at the table and a share in promises once reserved for the Israelites. The legal notice has already been signed and sent. Through Jesus the Messiah, God has accomplished this mission.

Paul declares that Jews and Gentiles have been drawn together by the blood of Jesus and that God now inhabits this diverse fellowship. The promises once limited to Abraham's descendants are now lavished on

---

[46] 3466, *mystērion* (μυστήριον): mystery, hidden, secret. It referred to a sacred, hidden secret, now revealed by God (Eph. 4:3-4, 6, 9). Mystery religions used it to speak of secrets known only by the initiated. Paul uses the term to describe how what was hidden in ages past (God's plan of salvation in Christ, the uniting of Jew and Gentile, the cosmic scope of redemption) is now revealed to the saints through the Spirit.

all who believe. Not even Paul's imprisonment can diminish his awe over this sweeping, eternal plan.

Paul writes not with despair but with wonder. Before he even finishes his prayer, he erupts in praise, marveling at the mystery of a new humanity. In Christ, God is forming a people not defined by race, history, or social status but by grace. God's new family is being built together as a living temple, a dwelling place for God Himself.

No Longer Jew vs. Greek

To appreciate the weight of this announcement, we need to understand the deep divide between Jews and Gentiles in the first century. Jews considered Gentiles to be unclean, and some would even wash their hands after Gentile contact, attempting to scrub away pagan "cooties." Meanwhile, many Greeks viewed others as culturally inferior. This mutual disdain formed the backdrop of the New Testament world.

In Jerusalem, the Court of the Gentiles in the temple was the only space where non-Jews could go. A stone inscription, written in Greek and Latin, warned that any Gentiles who crossed into the inner courts would have only themselves to blame for the death penalty that followed. The dividing wall was more than a metaphor. It was a visible, physical boundary.

Even among the earliest believers, unity was not automatic. Peter needed a rooftop vision in Acts 10 to realize God's welcome extended to Gentiles. Paul had to confront Peter in Galatians 2 when Peter, under social pressure, stopped eating with Gentile believers. For Paul to write that Jews and Gentiles are "fellow heirs" was nothing short of revolutionary. It was not merely religious theory. It was a call to dismantle centuries of ingrained separation.

Paul's gospel mission brought these worlds together. Jews and Gentiles were now worshiping, serving, and sharing life in the name of Christ. Paul did not see this as a problem but as the fulfillment of God's original design.

His prayer for this diverse group of believers was not that they would become the same but that they would become one in the love of Christ. People of every race, color, and class were being formed into one new family, God's household.[47] As Lewis Donelson put it, "Within the church of Jesus Christ, we belong to God's family, no matter what our race, clan, or tribe."[48]

I think of Bobby McDaniel, a longtime deacon who served on seven pastor-search committees during his years at our church. He once told me about a trip in the 1970s when the committee traveled to Laredo to hear a pastoral candidate preach. What stood out most was not the sermon but the congregation. The church was

---

47 Frances Foulkes, Ephesians: An Introduction and Commentary, Tyndale New Testament Commentaries 10 (Downers Grove, IL: InterVarsity Press, 2007), 93.

48 Lewis Donelson, Colossians, Ephesians, 1 and 2 Timothy and Titus (Louisville, KY: Westminster John Knox Press, 1996), 83.

about half Anglo and half Hispanic, something remarkably uncommon at the time.

On the long drive back to Weslaco, the group talked about what it would mean to reach the whole community with the gospel and how our church might begin to reflect the diversity of our city. At that time, Weslaco was predominantly Hispanic, while First Baptist was entirely Anglo.

That conversation planted seeds. Over time, the congregation made intentional efforts to bridge the cultural divide. Slowly, diversity took root. Today, our church family closely mirrors the demographics of our city. We are not a perfect congregation, but every time we gather as one body, we give thanks for the faithful vision of people like Bobby, who honored "the Father, from whom every family in heaven and on earth is named" (Eph. 3:14–15).[49]

The struggle for unity has marked every generation. During the civil rights movement, Dr. Martin Luther King Jr. famously said that 11:00 a.m. on Sunday was the most segregated hour in America.[50] That stinging indictment was true then, and in many places, it is still true today.

---

[49] G3965, *patria* (πατριά): family, lineage, clan; derived from *patēr* (father, G3962). Used for a group or community traced to a common father. Paul applies it in Eph. 3:15 to show that every family in heaven and on earth receives its name and identity from God the Father.

[50] Martin Luther King Jr., *Strength to Love* (New York: Harper & Row, 1963), 190.

That's My Brother

During a recent, painful season of racial unrest in our country, I called Charles Armstrong, a longtime African American member of our fellowship, to seek his perspective. I asked how we might do a better job of understanding and welcoming every member of our community. Charles responded with the grace and wisdom that marked his life. "Preacher," he said, "we have to learn to listen to each other and love each other with the love of Jesus." In an age when we tend to surround ourselves with people who think, vote, and talk like us, that is a tall order, but it is an essential one.

Two friends in our church clashed on Facebook. Their exchange was heated and unproductive. (There is a meme that says, "'Your passionate argument on Facebook changed my mind,' said no one, ever.") But months later, I saw those same two men sharing a meal at a church fellowship, talking, laughing, and focusing on Jesus instead of politics. That is the kind of transformation Paul envisioned: ordinary people crossing divides because of Christ.

That is our purpose. We are to show the world what life looks like in God's kingdom of grace, a kingdom without borders or boundaries. Some are hesitant to talk about these issues in church. Paul was not. Paul believed the church should lead, rather than lag behind, in demonstrating what redeemed humanity looks like.

When my son Nathan was a little sports-loving boy, he would spend hours in the backyard imagining himself scoring the winning touchdown in the Super Bowl. He would toss the ball to himself, run down the "field," and even provide his own play-by-play commentary. One afternoon, Lisa watched as he dove into the end zone for the imaginary game-winning score. She heard him shout with all the enthusiasm of a professional announcer, "Nathaaaan Rod-riguezzzz is in for the score!"

For the record, Nathan's last name is Parker. The Rodriguez family were dear friends from church. Their son, Noe Jr., was six years older than Nathan and a talented athlete he admired. In Nathan's mind, taking on the Rodriguez name was the highest compliment he could give himself, a way of stepping into the shoes of someone he looked up to.

Just a few weeks ago, I got a call from Noe Sr. to check in. In the middle of our conversation, he asked warmly, "How's my *sobrino* Nathan doing?" *Sobrino* is Spanish for "nephew." Noe sees himself as my brother in Christ, and that makes Nathan his nephew. What a beautiful image of the redeemed, barrier-defying family of Jesus! In Christ, we are not just acquaintances or teammates. We belong to one another. We take on each other's joys, bear each other's burdens, and celebrate each other's victories, not because we share the same bloodline but because we share the same Savior.

When we see each other this way, it changes how we live. It shapes the way we talk, forgive, and serve. It reminds us that God's grace builds a family that crosses every cultural and personal divide.

Spiritual Practice: See the Brother

Think of a fellow Christian you tend to see as "other." It may be someone whose politics anger you, whose background confuses you, or whose presence makes you uncomfortable. It could be someone from another cultural group, a different denomination, or a social circle that feels distant from yours. Write down their name (or initials), and underneath it, write this prayer:

- "Lord, help me see __________ the way You do.
- Help me say with Paul, and with faith, 'That's my brother' or 'That's my sister.'"

This week, look for one small way to build a bridge. It could be a kind word, a text message, an invitation to coffee, or simply listening with grace. It may feel awkward at first, but that is how family life begins, not in grand gestures, but in simple acts of kindness repeated over time.

Remember, the same Spirit who reconciled Jew and Gentile is still at work. He delights to bring strangers into the same household of faith, not just to coexist under one roof but to truly belong to one another. Each time you choose to see the image of God in someone you once viewed with suspicion or distance, you are living out the manifold wisdom of God. You are showing heaven and earth what grace looks like with skin on it.

Breakthrough Praise

That kind of radical, undeserved, and grace-fueled unity is what Paul longs for as he bows his knees. Throughout this chapter, he prays that believers would be strengthened in their inner being by God's Spirit, that Christ would make His home in their hearts, and that they would be rooted and grounded in love (Eph. 3:16–17).

Only in deep, daily communion with God can we begin to grasp "the breadth and length and height and depth" of His love. Only then can we truly know "the love of Christ that surpasses knowledge" and be filled "with all the fullness of God" (Eph. 3:18–19).

Paul concludes his prayer with a soaring doxology: "Now to him who is able to do far more abundantly than all that we ask or think, according to the power at work within us, to him be glory in the church and in Christ Jesus throughout all generations, forever and ever" (Eph. 3:20–21).

These words are not abstract theology to Paul. They are the heartbeat of his ministry and the anchor of his hope. Paul has seen God reconcile enemies, overturn centuries of prejudice, and build friendships where there was once only suspicion. If God could do that in the volatile, multicultural world of the first century, He can do it in ours.

Living Like Heirs

That is the kind of family Paul says we have been brought into, not by accident and not by merit, but by the deliberate will of God. The papers have been signed. The seal has been set. The estate is already ours in Christ. The moment we received the gospel, we were forgiven and adopted into God's family.

But adoption is only the beginning. Anyone who has walked through the process of welcoming a child into their home knows there is joy in the legal declaration, but there is also the day-to-day work of learning how to be family together. There are moments of misunderstanding, awkward conversations, and habits that must be unlearned. There are also moments of laughter, shared meals, and the quiet knowledge that, despite the differences, love is what makes a family.

In the same way, God has declared us brothers and sisters in Christ. Now we must learn to live like it. We must take the awkward first steps toward each other, even when we do not know the right words. We must show up for each other's celebrations and sorrows. We must be willing to be inconvenienced for the sake of love.

Where I worship each Sunday, we celebrate the dreams of those who longed for a more unified church, one that reflected the diversity of the Rio Grande

Valley. God honored that dream, and we have been blessed by it. Our congregation has members whose first languages are different, whose cultural traditions vary, and whose life experiences span everything from rural farming to city living. We are learning that being the family of God means not just sitting in the same sanctuary but standing together in the storms of life and rejoicing together in seasons of blessing.

This is what Paul envisioned when he wrote from prison about the manifold wisdom of God being made known through the church. Our unity is not an accident of geography or a coincidence of preference. It is the work of the Holy Spirit. It is a testimony to the watching world and to the rulers and authorities in heavenly places.

We are coheirs of this gospel. We are transformed by the good news of Jesus that shatters boundaries. Jews and Gentiles, Anglos and Hispanics, Black and white, male and female, rich and poor, old and young, are all brought together by the blood of Jesus. That grace invites us to dream big. We do so not because we are great but because God is. He can do more than we ask or imagine. Sometimes He even uses our suffering to change the world.

So let us live as heirs. Let us walk into the family home with gratitude and humility. Let us take our seat at the table, making room for the next brother or sister who arrives. Let us carry the family name with honor, showing the world the love of the One who brought us in when we were outsiders.

Praying the Message

God of grace and glory, we praise You for the mystery now made known that, through Christ, we are one family and one body and share one inheritance. Thank You for tearing down the walls that once divided us and for calling us into a love that surpasses knowledge.

Strengthen us by Your Spirit. Root us in Your love. Help us to see others not through the lens of fear or difference but through the eyes of Christ who brings us together. May Your church reflect the beauty of Your wisdom, a diverse people united in grace, a family that refuses to be divided along ethnic and racial lines, a dwelling where You are pleased to live.

Now to You, who are able to do far more than all we ask or imagine, be glory in the church and in Christ Jesus throughout all generations, forever and ever. Amen.

Further Reflection

Ephesians 3

1. **Context Connection**

   Paul, once a fierce persecutor of the church, was transformed on the road to Damascus and called to proclaim that the grace of God through Jesus is now available to all who call on His name. Gentiles are welcomed alongside Jewish believers as full heirs in God's kingdom.

- Have you ever experienced a moment in church that felt like a glimpse of this barrier-breaking unity?
- In a society defined by racial and cultural distrust, how can your church overcome such roadblocks to fellowship?

2. **Key Themes in the Text**

   The mystery revealed in Christ is that all believers, regardless of background, are fellow heirs, members of one body, and sharers in the promise of the gospel. In God's household, no one is a guest; all are adopted children with a place at the table and their picture on the family wall.

   - What does this truth reveal about God's heart for unity?
   - How does it challenge personal or cultural attitudes you have seen in the church?

3. **Church and Community Application**
   Paul's ministry and message call the church to embody reconciliation, diversity, and shared inheritance. This means crossing lines of language, culture, generation, and preference in practical ways. It means building real relationships, not just sharing a building.

   - What barriers still exist in your church or community that Christ's love can overcome?

- How might you take intentional steps to build a fellowship that reflects God's inclusive kingdom?

4. **Personal Transformation**
   Paul closes this section with a powerful doxology: *"Now to him who is able to do far more abundantly than all that we ask or think, according to the power at work within us…"* (Ephesians 3:20). This is not wishful thinking, but a declaration that the God who unites Jew and Gentile can still do what seems impossible in our lives today.

   - What are some bold prayers you have for your own spiritual growth or for your church?
   - How does trusting in God's power to work beyond what we imagine shape your hope?

5. **Closing Blessing or Prayer Prompt**
   Lord, thank You for breaking down the walls that divide us. Thank You for adopting us as Your children and giving us a shared inheritance in Christ. Help me to live in a way that reflects Your inclusive love and to dream boldly about what You can do in my life, in my church, and in my community. Amen.

Chapter 5

Balancing Our Call and Walk Ephesians 4:1-16

I therefore, a prisoner for the Lord, urge you to walk in a manner worthy of the calling to which you have been called, with all humility and gentleness, with patience, bearing with one another in love, eager to maintain the unity of the Spirit in the bond of peace.
(Ephesians 4:1-3)

Ones and Fives: Finding Balance

In college, exams told the truth about my study habits. At work, reality checks came during performance reviews. My friend Ray, a fellow pastor, likes to remind our staff during evaluations, "If all your scores are fives at work, you might be scoring ones at home."

It's a piercing way of saying what Paul is getting at here: balance matters.

If my kids graded me, most days I'd probably earn fives for paying the bills and getting them to school on time but might earn ones for telling too many "dad jokes" or making them wait while I finish another long meeting.

At a pastoral conference, someone once asked how I balance ministry and family. I told that person, "I don't." Balance isn't something you achieve once and keep forever; it's a moving target. Life rarely offers perfect equilibrium.

Instead, we live in a constant state of adjustment: shifting, recalibrating, getting it right, getting it wrong, and trying again. Some days one side feels heavier than the other. You may never feel like you've nailed it, but you keep aiming for balance.

That's the calling Paul sets forth in Ephesians 4: a life in which what we believe and how we live stay in step with one another.

Axios: A Life of Balance

At the heart of Paul's appeal is the Greek word *axios,*[51] translated "worthy." In Paul's world, *axios* meant "weighing as much; worth as much as."[52] Picture an

---

[51] G516, *axiōs* (ἀξίως): worthily, in a manner worthy of. For Paul this idea is not about *earning* worth but about *living in balance* with what God has already given. In Ephesians, the term captures the book's great theme: the harmony between doctrine (what God has done) and discipleship (how we live).

[52] Henry George Liddell et al., *A Greek-English Lexicon* (Oxford: Clarendon Press, 1996), 171.

old-fashioned scale: one side holds a fixed weight; the other must match it for the beam to level.

This call to balance didn't begin with Paul. The prophets had called Israel toward a life where belief and behavior met in the middle of God's will. Micah asks what the Lord requires, and the answer holds three weights that belong together: "do justice, love mercy, and walk humbly with your God" (Micah 6:8, author's rendering).

Any of those qualities alone would be insufficient for reflecting the spirit of our just and merciful God who revealed Himself fully through Jesus. Justice without mercy becomes harsh; mercy without justice turns careless. Humility grounds both justice and mercy in God, guiding us toward Christlike service. Taken together, in balance, these qualities fulfill the Lord's requirement for faithful living.

Paul's opening virtues in Ephesians 4 sound like Micah's ancient chord played again: humility, gentleness, patience, bearing with one another in love, and eager to maintain unity. The worthy walk is not a sprint of personal achievement. It is a steady gait where justice acts, mercy embraces, and humility keeps our steps light and teachable.

Israel's sages even warned about imbalance in a literal sense. Proverbs says: "A false balance is an abomination to the LORD, but a just weight is his delight" (Prov. 11:1 ESV). God is pleased with scales that tell the truth.

That's true in our business dealings, and it's true in our spiritual lives. When our doctrine says, "Christ is Lord," but our patterns at home, school, or work do not reflect His reign, the scale is lying. When our service in the community is generous, but we drift from the truth of the gospel, the scale deceives in the other direction.

Paul has already placed the fixed weight on one side, the staggering reality of chapters 1–3. Now he urges us to keep the other side, our walk, in balance.[53]

We were chosen before the creation of the world, adopted into God's family, redeemed through Jesus's own blood, made alive with Christ, sealed by the Spirit, and reconciled both to God and to one another. All this flows from God's eternal plan to bring all things together under the authority of Jesus Christ. The command to live an *axios* life calls us to balance those beliefs with transformed behaviors in our daily life, relationships, priorities, and decisions. This balance happens at the intersection of doctrine and discipleship.

That's why the gospel can't be reduced to "getting saved" or "going to heaven." McKnight describes the gospel of the kingdom as not merely a plan of salvation but the proclamation that Jesus is Lord. The fitting response to this good news is allegiance, surrendering

---

[53] Peterson, *Practice Resurrection*, Kindle Page 393.

to His authority, aligning with His reign, and joining His body, the church.[54]

Our commitment doesn't always reflect that level of surrender. I remember a church member telling me on multiple occasions, "Pastor, if you ever need anything at all, call me, day or night." It sounded like the kind of open-handed commitment every pastor dreams of hearing.

A while later, I took him up on it and asked if he could serve in an important ministry role. He declined; there was a scheduling conflict. No problem. Months later, I called again about another opportunity and got the same answer. Over the years, I probably made that call four or five times. Each time, his promises echoed in my mind, but they rang hollow.

It wasn't that he disliked me or the church, it was just that "anything, day or night" had quietly become "anything, as long as it fits my calendar conveniently." His words and his walk didn't balance.

Paul calls us to equilibrium between our calling and conduct, and Jesus modeled that balance in how He engaged people, often adding just the right weight to the scale to reveal whether their lives were truly in step with God's kingdom.

---

[54] Scot McKnight, *The King Jesus Gospel: The Original Good News Revisited* (Grand Rapids, MI: Zondervan, 2011), 45.

Rich Young Ruler or Zacchaeus: Adjusting a Tilted Scale

One day Jesus met a man who looked perfectly balanced: young, wealthy, respected, and devout. He had the résumé of a model believer. But when he asked what more he needed to do, Jesus placed a different weight on the scale: "One thing you lack… sell what you have, give to the poor, then follow me" (Mark 10:21 NIV, slightly paraphrased).

The man walked away grieving. His life was heavy on morality and performance but light on kingdom surrender.

That's the danger Paul warns us about: we can appear balanced in religious activity yet lean dangerously when love, humility, or obedience are missing. If our scale is heavy with church involvement but light on Christlike love or full of biblical knowledge but lacking surrender, Jesus still calls, "Come, follow me and bring that part of your life that you're holding back."

Not everyone turned away when Jesus added a new weight to the scale. Shortly after Luke's account of the rich young ruler, we meet Zacchaeus, a wealthy tax collector whose life tilted heavily toward greed and self-interest.

When Jesus called Zacchaeus down from the sycamore tree and invited Himself to his home, Zacchaeus responded with joy and decisive action:

"Look, Lord! Here and now I give half of my possessions to the poor, and if I have cheated anybody… I will pay back four times the amount" (Luke 19:8 NIV, slightly paraphrased). His calling and his walk found alignment in a single afternoon.

The rich young ruler heard Jesus's call to count the cost and retreated to his comfortable life, full of grief because he knew he was missing what God wanted for him. Zacchaeus, on the other hand, responded with even greater enthusiasm than Jesus required: repenting and restoring with open hands.

Zacchaeus became the lost coin and lamb who were found. He lived the story of the prodigal who was embraced by the Father. In his repentance, we see the "camel pass through the eye of the needle" (Luke 18:25) as Jesus transformed his life and brought balance where there had been earthly wealth and heavenly poverty.

The rich young ruler and Zacchaeus are mirrors facing opposite directions. One had a spotless moral résumé but couldn't release his grip on possessions; the other probably had a history of dishonesty but gladly loosened his grip the moment Jesus called. One walked away sad. The other welcomed Jesus with joy. One let imbalance keep him from following; the other found balance by putting his feet in motion toward generosity and restitution.

Both men were invited into the kingdom. The difference wasn't how much they owned, but how much their hearts were willing to shift. And that's the invitation for us: to keep stepping back onto the scales and letting the Spirit adjust the weight until our confessions and our conduct match.

When that happens, it doesn't just shape our personal walks. It changes the way the whole church functions.

Gifted for Service

Jesus calls us into His church and equips us for service. Paul says that He gave the church apostles, prophets, evangelists, shepherds, and teachers, not so a few can do all the work, but to equip every believer for ministry and build up the body of Christ.

Apostles are sent ones who extend the gospel's reach.[55] Paul had this gift. Today it's seen in missionaries, church planters, and those who push us beyond our walls. A Canadian church planter preparing to start a Portuguese-speaking church in Vancouver rode the SkyTrain, striking up conversations whenever he heard Portuguese spoken. Within months, a congregation formed. That's an apostolic mission. Without apostles, a church grows stagnant; without depth, apostolic work becomes shallow.

Prophets speak God's truth with clarity and courage.[56] Prophetic voices are heard throughout the

---

[55] G652, *apostolos* (ἀπόστολος): apostle, commissioned messenger, delegate.

[56] G4396, *prophētēs* (προφήτης): prophet, one who speaks forth a message from God.

Scriptures. Modern prophets still call the church to be just and repent. They remind us to care for the poor, defend the unborn, and resist compromise. Without love, prophecy becomes harsh; without a prophetic voice, the church drifts toward God-dishonoring injustice or doctrinal error.

Evangelists share the gospel and invite others to follow Christ.[57] "Pastor, I met this family out in the parking lot, and they all just prayed to receive Christ. I'd like you to meet *hermano* Rodriguez and his family," my friend Lupe said in our church kitchen, grinning from ear to ear. Moments later, I was shaking hands with a smiling family whose lives had just been changed by the good news of Jesus. The gospel spread like wildfire in the first century through the work of the early evangelists and continues to advance today through the ongoing witness of faithful people like my friend Lupe. Without evangelists, the church turns inward. Without discipleship, new believers stall. Both are essential, and they must remain in balance.

Shepherds nurture, guide, and protect.[58] Jesus modeled this perfectly. When Lisa and I were interviewing for the first time with a pastoral search committee years ago, a woman asked her, "So, do you play the piano or sing or teach in the women's

---

[57] G2099, *euangelistēs* (εὐαγγελιστής): evangelist, bearer of good news, proclaimer of the gospel.

[58] G4166, *poimēn* (ποιμήν): shepherd, herdsman; metaphorically, one who tends, leads, and cares for a group of believers.

ministry?" Lisa replied humbly, "I don't play the piano, and I'm not very comfortable speaking or singing in front of a group. But I'm a good listener." Decades later, when we returned for the funeral of that woman's husband, she sat next to Lisa and, with tears in her eyes, said, "We've had a lot of pastor's wives since you all left. And they've all done lots of good things. But none of them have been good listeners." She was, in effect, saying, "Thanks for being a good shepherd." Our churches need a lot more of that.

Teachers explain God's Word so others can live it.[59] Faithful men and women fulfill this calling each week in Sunday School classes and small group settings across the globe. Some are doing it as they work through this book right now. That ministry sometimes leads faithful believers into service outside the church setting. My friend Bob led a Bible study in his dealership's breakroom for years, grounding coworkers in Scripture long after he could have retired. Teachers keep the church centered in God's truth, helping believers connect Scripture to their daily walk.

You don't have to be an apostle to seek new mission fields, a prophet to speak truth in love, an evangelist to pray for someone by name, a pastor to listen well, or a teacher to share what God has taught you. These gifts aren't limited to seminary-trained

---

[59] G1320, *didaskalos* (διδάσκαλος): teacher, instructor; one who imparts knowledge, especially in matters of faith and doctrine.

leaders; they show up in everyday people in everyday places. As Eddie Rasnake points out, "The bulk of ministry in a church is to be accomplished not by the leadership but by the laity."[60]

When our church needed help with media, my friend Izzy quietly said yes. That yes has turned into nearly two decades of behind-the-scenes faithfulness for his whole family. During the pandemic, they kept the church connected when we couldn't meet in person. They built up the body not from the stage or the classroom but from the sound booth.

That's Paul's vision: every part does its work in love. Every person matters. No role is too small.

Harmony in the Body

That kind of shared life of service keeps us on track and builds faithful rhythms into our fellowship as we learn to think more about others than about ourselves. I'll admit that I don't always keep in step with that selfless, Christlike cadence. One Sunday, I found myself out of sync.

A missionary from China came to speak. As we sang, I caught myself critiquing the music in my head. When she began, her first words stopped me: "What a blessing to sing out loud with you today. In China, we play secular music in the background to hide our praise

---

[60] Eddie Rasnake, *The Book of Ephesians*, 98.

from passersby." In an instant, my focus shifted from personal preference to kingdom gratitude.

We've had times since then when the music was off (just as I'm sure the sermon is off quite often), but I've never heard it the same way again. Now I hear it with the ears of someone who knows others would give anything to sing freely.

That conversation didn't just change my listening; it changed my leading. Since that Sunday, whenever I step into the pulpit or stand among the congregation during singing, I remember that somewhere, at that very moment, brothers and sisters are whispering their praise so authorities won't hear.

According to recent estimates, more than 360 million Christians worldwide face high levels of persecution and discrimination for their faith. Yet they still sing, gather, and open God's Word, even when it costs them dearly.

Their example reminds me that worship is not about flawless execution, perfect harmonies, or personal preference. It is about giving glory to the One who is worthy and makes us worthy, even if the song is off-key or muttered quietly.

But harmony, in music or in the body of Christ, is fragile. It takes more than good intentions to keep it. Paul knew how easily the notes could drift apart, and that's why he gave us both a goal to aim for and a warning to heed.

Avoiding Imbalance: Truth in Love

When Paul calls us to speak *the truth*[61] *in love,*[62] he isn't offering a polite suggestion. He's warning us about a real danger: loveless truth and truthless love. I've seen both kinds of failures play out in church business meetings, family living rooms, and countless other places. Wherever we see them, these extremes are destructive.

A family that focuses exclusively on truth usually fosters cold, lifeless relationships. One that emphasizes love without truth has a shallow bond that is easily broken. A church heavy on truth but light on love can quote Scripture flawlessly while freezing people out with its tone. A church heavy on love but light on truth can throw the warmest potlucks while quietly letting sin and error eat away at its foundation.

The answer isn't to aim for some bland halfway point; it's to live in the fullness of both: truth spoken in love and love anchored in truth.

I remember sitting in a meeting when a church leader stood and angrily condemned certain groups in our society who were, in his view, "destroying America." Across the room, I noticed an elderly

---

61 G225, *alētheia* (ἀλήθεια): truth, reality, that which is in accord with fact and God's nature.

62 G26, *agapē* (ἀγάπη): love, goodwill, benevolence. Refers most fully to God's unconditional, self-giving love revealed in Christ, but also to the love believers show toward God and others as they reflect His character (Eph. 5:2; 1 John 4:7–11).

woman quietly wiping away tears. Her son had contracted AIDS after years of living outside God's design for human sexuality. She and her husband disagreed with his sinful choices but had spent months caring for him and his partner in their weakened states, showing Jesus's love through acts of compassion and grace. Not wanting to bring shame to his family, the son had arranged to be buried far from home. Years later, his mother had his body exhumed and brought back to the family plot. I officiated that reburial service only a few days before the leader's harsh words caused her tears to fall.

That man had an important point to make, but this particular Sunday might not have been the best moment for it, given what was happening in our small fellowship that weekend. His words, intended to defend truth, landed without love. In that instant, the gap between truth and love wasn't theological or moral; it was a wound in the heart of a grieving mother. Though they held the same convictions, his tone and timing drove a wedge where a touch of grace and sympathy could have built connection. Moments like that remind me why Paul weds truth to love: because without both, the body stops functioning as Christ intended.

It's not God-honoring when a church's response to the world's brokenness is an unloving, wagging finger. Nor is it God-honoring to turn a blind eye to blatant sin. True love tells the truth, and true grace never conceals injustice.

An extreme example of the failure to live this way is when churches ignore reports of sexual misconduct and abuse, quietly allowing predators to move into unsuspecting communities. In such moments, saying "We all just need to forgive and get along" is not the gospel's answer. To forgive doesn't dissolve the consequences of one's actions. These situations call for forgiveness and require a "thus saith the LORD" prophetic word grounded in God's righteousness and, when necessary, the involvement of law enforcement. Faithfulness to the gospel requires the courage to speak the truth in love and act accordingly.

At other times, we are called to address less egregious but still spiritually dangerous patterns. On many occasions as both a father and a pastor, I've had to say, "I love you too much not to say something about this." Those conversations were not easy; sometimes they brought tears, sometimes frustration, and sometimes long silences. But love that never risks discomfort isn't really love at all.

In this age where both biblical truth and God-honoring kindness seem to be in short supply, we need courageous conversations like that in our homes and churches. We need to uphold biblical values while modeling unfailing, sacrificial, and Christlike grace. Living a balanced life of faith that speaks the truth in love often means having discussions that make us squirm. In the end, those discussions tend to draw us closer to each other and to the heart of our loving, just, and merciful God.

The only way to hold that tension is to stay connected to Christ. He is the Head, the Source from whom the whole body grows. He joins and holds us together, building us up in love as each part does its work (Eph. 4:16 ESV).

Spiritual Practice: Balance Audit, A Calling and Walk Self-Check

When Christ is the anchor, the whole church grows in harmony, but that harmony begins with each part of the body doing its work. The balance scale isn't only for the church as a whole; it's for you and me. Paul's vision for truth and love isn't an abstract ideal for leaders' meetings or mission statements. It's a daily call for all believers to weigh their own lives in light of the gospel.

Take a quiet moment with the scale image in your mind and prayerfully evaluate these areas. Give yourself a rating from 1 (needs much growth) to 5 (healthy and aligned):

- Worship: Do my habits reflect God's worth?
- Relationships: Am I humble, gentle, and patient?
- Service: Am I using my gifts to build up others?
- Integrity: Does my private life match my public faith?

- Generosity: Do my resources serve kingdom priorities?
- Witness: Am I pointing others to Jesus?

Praying the Message

Lord, You have called me by Your grace and given me a place in Your body. Teach me to walk in a way that reflects that calling. Help my words and my life to weigh the same on Your scale. Keep me from leaning into truth without love or love without truth. Make me a person whose conduct matches my confession and make us a church whose conduct matches our confession. Amen.

Further Reflection

Ephesians 4:1-16

1. **Context Connection**
   Paul writes from prison, urging believers to live in a way that matches the calling they have received. His language is deeply communal, envisioning a church united in purpose, gifted for ministry, and growing together toward maturity in Christ.

   - How might Paul's imprisonment have shaped the urgency and passion of his appeal for unity and maturity in the church?

   - What connections do you see between Paul's vision of a united church in Ephesians 4 and the challenges your church faces today?

2. **Key Themes in the Text**

   Paul uses the Greek word *axios* to picture a scale in balance, with one side holding the weight of God's calling and the other our daily walk. He also lists the gifts Christ gives the church to help it grow in love and truth.

   - What does it mean for your "calling" and your "walk" to be in balance?
   - Which of the gifts listed in verses 11–12 have you seen most clearly at work in your church? How have they shaped your growth?

3. **Church and Community Application**

   Paul warns against the dangers of imbalance—truth without love or love without truth—and calls the church to speak the truth in love so that the body grows in harmony.

   - Where have you seen truth and love working together in a way that brought healing or growth to the church?
   - What steps could your congregation take to better equip every believer for ministry?

4. **Personal Transformation**

   Living in balance requires ongoing self-examination and Spirit-led adjustment. Paul's picture of the body "joined and held together" depends on each part doing its work.

- Which area of your life feels most "out of balance" with your calling right now?
- How might God be inviting you to use your gifts to build up the body of Christ this week?

5. **Closing Blessing or Prayer Prompt**
   May the Lord align your calling and your walk so that your life reflects the truth and love of Christ, and may He equip you to strengthen His body in every word and deed.

CHAPTER 6

THROWING OFF OUR GRAVE CLOTHES EPHESIANS 4:17–32

. . . to put off your old self, which belongs to your former manner of life and is corrupt through deceitful desires, and to be renewed in the spirit of your minds, and to put on the new self, created after the likeness of God in true righteousness and holiness.
(Ephesians 4:22–24)

I packed a duffel bag with thrift-store clothes for a mission trip in the mountains of Virginia because I knew the work would be messy. After a long day covered in mud, Sheetrock dust, and fiberglass, I returned so filthy that Lisa wouldn't even let me step inside the mission dormitory where we were staying. She hosed me down with ice-cold mountain water before I crossed the threshold (I think she enjoyed that chore immensely). Some of those clothes were ruined and had to be thrown away. They were beyond washing.

That is Paul's picture of the old self. Some garments of our past cannot be patched up but must be discarded. We cannot wear those clothes into the life of Christ.

At this point in the letter, Paul makes a decisive shift. In the first half of Ephesians, he proclaimed the gospel's foundation: who God is and what God has done in Christ. Now his focus turns to us: how we live in response to that reality. Before Christ, we were "dead in our trespasses[63] and sins."[64] But God, rich in mercy, "made us alive together with Christ" (Eph. 2:1–6).

Salvation was not the finish line. It was the starting line of a new life. In the preceding section, Paul pictured this balanced conversation about life and salvation with the word *axios*, suggesting a scale holding together our calling and our walk. Now he presses us to live that balance out by throwing off the old and putting on the new.

Out with the Old, in with the New

The story of Lazarus sharpens the image. When Jesus called him from the tomb, he shuffled out still wrapped

---

[63] G3900, *paraptōma* (παράπτωμα): trespass, lapse, deviation, transgression. The term can mean "slip," "blunder," or "error that is either unintentional or deliberate." In a moral / theological sense, it refers to a violation of God's standards (Eph. 2:1).

[64] G266, *hamartia* (ἁμαρτία): missing the mark, failure, error. It means "failure to hit the target, making a mistake, or engaging in wrongdoing." In a moral / theological sense it refers to falling short of God's standard (Eph. 2:1).

in grave clothes. The smell of death clung to him. Jesus could have removed the wrappings Himself, but instead He told the community, "Unbind him, and let him go." Resurrection life is meant to be lived free, and sometimes it takes the help of others to peel away what no longer belongs.

The truth is that grave clothes cling tightly. They are habits, wounds, and shame that bind us. Paul commands us to "put off the old self" (4:22) and "put on the new self" (4:24). Like Lazarus, we have been raised; like my ruined work clothes, the old life must be thrown away.

There is a striking difference between Lazarus and Jesus. Lazarus was raised back into mortal life, still bound in strips of cloth. Jesus rose into glorified life, His burial garments left neatly folded in the tomb (John 20:6–7). We live between those two stories. Like Lazarus, we have been raised, but the old wrappings still cling. We long for the day when all that is mortal will be clothed in glory, like Jesus.

Renewed Minds, New Desires

Why do the old wrappings cling so tightly? Because sin deceives us. It promises freedom but delivers slavery. It whispers of satisfaction but leaves us emptier than before. Consumerism promises contentment while leaving us restless. Sexual sin promises intimacy while eroding it. Workaholism promises worth and respect while hollowing us out. Over time, repeated behaviors carve deep ruts in our minds until they feel inevitable.

This is why Paul says we must "be renewed in the spirit of our minds" (Eph. 4:23). The gospel does not simply tell us to try harder. The Spirit rewires us from the inside out, shaping new desires and new thought patterns until the likeness of God is formed in us.

And the good news is that we do not fight this battle alone. Christ has raised us to new life. His Spirit is within us. And His people stand ready to help us strip away the grave clothes and put on garments of grace.

So, the question becomes this: What grave clothes are you still carrying? What habits, attitudes, or secret shames are keeping you bound? You do not have to wear them anymore. In Christ, you have been raised to new life. His Spirit and His people are ready to help you throw them away and put on the garments of grace.

The New Walk: Living in Resurrection Reality

This is what Paul means by walking in balance. Our calling is new life in Christ, and our daily walk is the shedding of what no longer belongs.

After laying out the breathtaking truths of the gospel, Paul shifts abruptly to practical instruction. His blunt contrast between the Christian walk and the world's ways may feel jarring, but it is the natural result of resurrection life. Because of Christ's saving work, believers are called to a radically new way of living.

We step out of the garments of death and into resurrection life. That means abandoning the darkness and futility of our former ways. Sensuality, greed, and impurity no longer belong among God's people (Eph. 4:17–19).

Instead of clinging to falsehood, we are to speak truth (Eph. 4:25). Instead of flying off the handle, Paul calls us to be angry without sinning and to deal with anger before sundown (Eph. 4:26–27). A follower of Jesus who once stole must now find honest work—not just for self-sufficiency but for generosity (Eph. 4:28). Honest labor enables us to help those in need.

In God's family, corrupting talk must be replaced with words that build others up (Eph. 4:29). Words can either poison or heal a community. Paul calls us to choose the latter.

Then comes a tender warning: *"Do not grieve the Holy Spirit of God, by whom you were sealed for the day of redemption"* (Eph. 4:30). Clarence Jordan's *Cotton Patch Gospel* captures the emotional weight of this command: *"Don't wring the heart of God's Holy Spirit, who stamped his OK on you on your Emancipation Day."* [65] This is not about legalistic morality but about a relationship. The Spirit is not a distant force but a present companion who shares in our joys and sorrows.

Paul's reminder is deeply personal. When we lie, we wound the Spirit of truth. When we speak with bitterness, we sadden the Spirit of grace. When we harbor unforgiveness, we resist the Spirit who has

[65] Clarence Jordan, *The Cotton Patch Gospel* (Macon, GA: Smyth & Helwys Publishing, 2004), Eph. 4:29.

forgiven us in Christ. But when we forgive, when we show kindness, and when we choose words that give life, we bring joy to the Spirit who dwells within us.

Holiness is not about appearances. It is about nurturing a relationship with the God who has made His home in our hearts. Every choice of bitterness, deception, or rage breaks relational trust. But every act of kindness, compassion, and forgiveness echoes God's own heart and brings Him joy.

Paul's list of holy exchanges that mark resurrection living is striking:

- Lies must give way to truth.
- Anger must be controlled and resolved.
- Stealing must be replaced with generosity.
- Corrupt words must give way to grace-filled speech.
- Bitterness must be exchanged for kindness and forgiveness.

These are not lofty ideals. They are daily, practical ways of living out our faith in a broken world.

The grave clothes come off, and the garments of mercy go on. Clothed in Christ, we walk daily in righteousness, truth, and forgiveness. And we do not wear these garments in our own strength, but by the Spirit who empowers us to live in resurrection life.[66]

---

[66] Peterson, *Practice Resurrection,* Kindle Page 267–68.

I once saw this casting aside of grave clothes happen in the middle of a worship service. Two women on our worship team had been in conflict. One Sunday, as we sang, one set down her instrument and walked toward the other. Overcome with emotion, the other stopped playing. Tears flowed as they embraced. Forgiveness was offered, and grace filled the room. It was resurrection life breaking in before our eyes.

Historical and Cultural Background: Ephesus

The believers in Ephesus faced a different but equally powerful struggle. Their city was a hub of trade, politics, and pagan worship. At the city's center stood the massive temple of Artemis (Diana), one of the seven wonders of the ancient world. More than a religious site, it was a cultural and economic powerhouse where fertility rituals, superstition, and temple prostitution thrived. Religion was transactional: you paid the goddess for protection, prosperity, or fertility.

When Paul preached the gospel in Ephesus, he was calling men and women out of a society where greed, sensuality, and idolatry weren't just tolerated; they were celebrated. Imagine standing in Times Square with all its lights and noise—only every billboard glorifies sin. That was the daily environment for Ephesian believers.

Finding Common Values in Christ

Paul's tone here is blunt. After the soaring theology of the first half of Ephesians, his instructions in chapter 4 are direct. Most of these believers were coming to Christ out of paganism, not Judaism. They had no shared moral foundation, no biblical tradition to guide them. Paul had to lay out the basics of a God-honoring life.

I was reminded of this in a premarital counseling session years ago. When I asked about sexual ethics, a young woman admitted that no one had ever spoken to her about what Scripture teaches. She had simply followed cultural norms. That moment underscored the importance of candid conversations with those under our care. We cannot assume people know the story of Scripture. Often, we must start from the ground up.

Paul does the same with the Ephesian believers. He spells out a new way of life and anchors it in grace: "Therefore…" he begins. That one word ties everything together. We do not live a holy life to earn God's favor. We live a holy life because God has already lavished us with grace.

A New Wardrobe

As we put off the old garments of sin, Paul invites us to step into something entirely new: garments tailored in righteousness. This wardrobe is not off-the-rack morality, but a custom-made life stitched with mercy, grace, and truth.

This isn't only about changing habits. It's about receiving a whole new way of being. Mercy replaces malice, truth replaces deceit, and forgiveness replaces bitterness. And we don't wear these garments in our own strength but through the Spirit who empowers us to walk in resurrection life.

Later in the New Testament, Jesus dictates a letter to this same church in Ephesus, warning them that they had "forsaken the love they had at first" (Rev. 2:4). Paul saw that temptation coming. He knew believers might drift, tempted to trade garments of grace for rags of sin. We face the same temptation today.

But Paul's call is not just to believe in the risen Jesus; it is to be clothed in His character day by day. Transformation is not a one-time event but a daily renewal, a deliberate "putting on" of the new self.

Francis of Assisi knew this well. The son of a wealthy merchant, he stripped off his fine clothes in the public square and chose instead to be clothed in simplicity for Christ. Out of that surrender flowed a movement of renewal that still shapes the church today.

John Newton, once a hardened slave trader, was transformed by grace and spent his life preaching mercy. His hymn "Amazing Grace" still testifies to being rescued from blindness.

Corrie Ten Boom, after surviving a Nazi concentration camp, traveled to preach forgiveness. At one gathering she recognized a former guard. In her own strength she could not forgive, but as she prayed, 'Jesus, help me," Christ's power enabled her to embrace him. Her story reminds us that forgiveness is not natural; it is supernatural. Only the Spirit of Christ can empower us to extend mercy where everything in us screams for revenge.

Corrie Ten Boom's story shows how only the Spirit can clothe us with forgiveness when our own strength fails. That same truth still inspires believers to live this transformation and to express it in art and song. My friend Ray captured it beautifully in the lyrics to his original song:

"Throw Off Your Grave Clothes"

Written by Raymond Sanchez

You knitted me together
in my mother's womb
Since that time I was heading down
To a fiery tomb

Life was stitched with sadness
Lining sewed with gloom
Stench of death was on my clothes
Till Jesus called me out of that tomb

So I threw off my grave clothes
And put on the new line
Made by the Savior
Bought with the blood of Christ

I'll throw off my old self
Put on a new mind
Clothed in compassion
Sharing the love of Christ

Your life may be unraveling
Garments stained with sin
Holdin' on just by a thread
Not knowing where to begin

Clothes all stripped and tattered
Your fabric wearing thin
But there's a Label filled with life
If you let the Savior in!

And throw off your grave clothes
Put on the new line
Made by the Savior
Bought with the blood of Christ

So throw off your old self
Put on a new mind
Clothed in compassion
Sharing the love of Christ

I've heard it said you are who you wear
but also how you dress
So if you're dressing well, my friend,
you wear the best

Clothed in compassion
Sharing the love of Christ[67]

(Listen to "Throw Off Your Grave Clothes" and find other helpful resources here:

67 Raymond Sanchez, "Throw Off Your Grave Clothes," unpublished lyrics. Lyrics used by permission of the copyright holder. All rights reserved.

https://www.drstevenparker.com/getting-the-church-inside-you-resources.)

As you reflect on these truths, don't rush past them. Let the Spirit show you what you still need to take off and what Christ wants you to put on. This isn't self-help; it's surrender.

Ask yourself: *What do I need to leave behind at the tomb? What would it look like to walk forward in resurrection life this week?*

So let the grave clothes fall. And walk forward, clothed in Christ.

Spiritual Practice: Putting Off and Putting On

Paul's words invite us to practice resurrection in the daily rhythm of our lives: *"Put off your old self… be renewed… put on the new self"* (Eph. 4:22–24). One simple way to step into this rhythm is through a short evening reflection.

1. **Put Off: Confess the Old**
   - Where today did I slip back into the old self?
   - Recall moments of impatience, dishonesty, or words that tore others down.
   - Lay them before God, trusting His mercy.
2. **Be Renewed: Receive the Spirit**
   - Sit quietly in God's presence. Invite the Spirit to refresh your heart and mind.

- Slowly read Ephesians 4:30–32, letting words like *kindness* and *forgiveness* soak in.

3. **Put On: Step into the New**
   - How do I want to walk differently tomorrow?
   - Pray for grace to speak truth, act generously, and forgive freely.
   - Choose one small action for the next day that reflects new life in Christ.

This rhythm of confession, renewal, and recommitment helps us live what Paul describes. It is not about perfection but about practicing resurrection.

The Christian life is not about managing appearances. It is about being made new in Christ. Each day we are invited to cast off what no longer fits and to be clothed in mercy, truth, and love. This is the freedom of the gospel: not merely freedom to exist but to walk in resurrection life as God's beloved children.

Praying the Message

Lord Jesus, thank You for calling me out of the grave. Help me leave behind bitterness, fear, shame, and sin. Clothe me in Your mercy, and teach me to walk in grace, truth, and forgiveness. May my life reflect Your love and bring joy to Your heart through the Spirit within me. Amen.

Further Reflection

Ephesians 4:17-32

1. **Context Connection**
   Paul contrasts the futility of life apart from God with the transformed life of those who follow Christ. To a Gentile audience unfamiliar with God's story, he spells out what it means to "put off" the old self and "put on" the new. His final instruction is both profound and practical: *"Forgive one another, as God in Christ forgave you"* (Eph. 4:32).

   - What does Paul mean by this clothing imagery of putting off and putting on?
   - How does this shift affect your daily attitudes, speech, and relationships?

2. **Key Themes in the Text**
   Forgiveness is central to new life in Christ. It is not based on feelings but on the willful choice to extend mercy as we have received it. Paul also highlights truth-telling, Spirit-led renewal, and speech that builds up rather than tears down.

   - How does God's forgiveness in Christ inspire your own acts of mercy?
   - Why do you think Paul connects forgiveness with unity in the church?

3. **Church and Community Application**
   Paul envisions a community where truth is spoken in love, anger is handled without sin, and generosity replaces selfishness.
   - How would your church's witness change if its members forgave others as consistently as Christ has forgiven you?
   - What habits or conversations could help your fellowship embody these values?
4. **Personal Transformation**
   Forgiveness often requires relinquishing the right to get even and trusting God with justice.
   - Who comes to mind when you hear Paul's call to forgive as God forgave you?
   - How might the Holy Spirit help you take the next step toward forgiveness and reconciliation?
5. **Closing Blessing**
   Lord, thank You for the forgiveness we have received in Christ. Help us release bitterness, speak words that give grace, and live together in the freedom of Your mercy. Amen.

CHAPTER 7

GROWING INTO OUR FATHER'S CLOTHES EPHESIANS 5:1-21

Therefore be imitators of God, as beloved children. And walk in love, as Christ loved us and gave himself up for us, a fragrant offering and sacrifice to God. (Ephesians 5:1-2)

I first remember needing to dress up for something that required a sport coat when I was about thirteen or fourteen. I can't recall whether it was a school presentation or a 4-H or FFA event, but whatever it was, it came up suddenly, and I didn't have the right clothes. I put on a freshly ironed button-up shirt, borrowed one of my dad's ties (which he tied for me), and then slipped into one of his sport coats.

My mom oohed and aahed about how grown-up I looked, so I stepped in front of the mirror to see for myself. What I saw wasn't a future CEO but a skinny kid swimming in his dad's jacket. Through "mom goggles," I might have looked like I was ready to lead a

Fortune 500 company. Through my eyes, I looked like what I was, a kid in clothes that didn't quite fit yet.

When my kids were small, they used to sleep in my T-shirts. Those makeshift sleep shirts swallowed them up like oversized gowns. They loved it. It was fun, and probably cozy, to wear something a thousand sizes too big. My kids would never have left the house dressed like that, but they had a blast running around in something so consuming.

Lately, those memories have come back to me often, especially after my dad passed away. Not long after his death, my mom gave me a stack of his shirts. Getting dressed in the morning can feel emotional when I put one on, but it also makes my heart glad. The shirts bring back memories of better times, before life wore him down, before he lost the strength to enjoy the world the way he once did.

And here's the thing I've noticed: the shirts fit now. I'm no longer the awkward teenager who looked out of place in his dad's jacket. I've grown into them. I have a wife and kids, a mortgage, a job, and all the responsibilities of adulthood. I understand more of what my dad must have felt when life was heavy, and I was just a teenager trying to make sense of the world. I hope I've grown into the kind of man who would make him proud. And I hope that one day my kids will look at me the way I looked at him.

Mimicking Our Heavenly Father

Paul exhorted the believers in and around Ephesus to "be imitators of God, as beloved children" (Ephesians 5:1). In modern usage, the word *imitation* often carries a negative connotation. We think of fake products like an imitation Rolex or a knockoff designer bag. Or we remember an annoying little sibling echoing every word we said, driving us up the wall.

But in the Greco-Roman world of Paul's day, imitation was seen as a mark of respect. To imitate someone was to acknowledge that person's excellence and seek to pattern one's life after that person's life. It was viewed as a noble calling, a deliberate pursuit of moral and spiritual formation shaped by worthy examples.[68]

The Greek word translated "imitators" is *mimētai*,[69] from which we get the English word *mimic*, meaning "to act like, to mirror."[70] As Kenneth Wuest explains, the term conveys the idea of "becoming a pattern of another's behavior," highlighting deliberate and

[68] Walter L. Liefeld, *Ephesians*, The IVP New Testament Commentary Series 10 (Downers Grove, IL: InterVarsity Press, 1997), 143.

[69]G3402, *Mimētēs* (μιμητής): "an imitator, follower," from *mimeomai*, "to imitate." From this root we derive the English words *mimic* and *mime*.

[70] Max Anders, *Galatians, Ephesians, Philippians, Colossians*, Holman New Testament Commentary 8 (Nashville, TN: Broadman & Holman Publishers, 1999), 170.

sustained imitation rather than casual resemblance.[71] The *Cotton Patch Gospel* captures this well: "Therefore, become God's mimics, like children who are dearly loved."[72] *The Message* puts it even more plainly: "Watch what God does, and then you do it, like children who learn proper behavior from their parents."[73] That's the image Paul gives us, children watching their parent closely, learning by example.

When we think about mimicking our Father in heaven (watching and doing what God does) it becomes clear just how much growing we still have to do. We're like that teenager in a sport coat that doesn't quite fit yet. Or even more so, like four-year-old children clomping around the house in T-shirts that reach their ankles.

Like small children who long to be like their parents, we want to be like our heavenly Father. But we know, deep down, that we still have a long way to go. We want to throw off the grave clothes of sin and death and put on the new wardrobe of righteousness, but sometimes those redeemed clothes feel like they would swallow us. We try them on, but they don't quite fit yet.

And that's okay.

---

[71] Kenneth S. Wuest, *Wuest's Word Studies from the Greek New Testament: For the English Reader* (Grand Rapids: Eerdmans, 1973), 1:131.

[72] Clarence Jordan, *The Cotton Patch Gospel*, Eph. 5:1.

[73] Eugene H. Peterson, *The Message: The Bible in Contemporary Language* (Colorado Springs: NavPress, 2005), Eph. 5:1.

Paul understood that discipleship is a process. Becoming imitators of God doesn't happen overnight. It's something we grow into, little by little, grace by grace, and step by step. Beginning in this next section of his letter, Paul shows us what it looks like to grow up in Christ. He paints a vision of what it means to wear our Father's shirt and finally have it fit.

Christlike Love in Action

Christlike love is the great theme of the New Testament. It begins with the initiating love of Christ. Jesus's love is self-giving and sacrificial. Paul makes it plain that imitating God means walking in this kind of love: "as Christ loved us and gave himself up for us, a fragrant offering and sacrifice to God" (Eph. 5:2 ESV).

If we want to know what God's love looks like, we must look to Jesus. His life, death, and resurrection reveal a love that costs. We are called to practice that same love daily, in all our relationships.

This isn't sentimental or abstract. It is tangible love, a love that reshapes how we live, moves us to serve others, and realigns our hearts with the heart of God. Jesus modeled this by pouring out His life for ours. Now we are invited to imitate that pattern: love answering love, made possible by the initiating grace of Christ.[74]

---

[74] Francis Foulkes, *Ephesians: An Introduction and Commentary*, Tyndale New Testament Commentaries 10 (Downers Grove, IL: InterVarsity Press, 1989), 144–5.

The Greek word here for love is *agape,*[75] a word that carries the sense of a deep, self-giving, covenantal love that seeks the good of the other. It is not a vague emotion or fleeting affection. It is costly, sacrificial love that reshapes relationships, refines motives, and reorients our hearts toward others.[76]

President John F. Kennedy once inspired Americans with the challenge: "Ask not what your country can do for you; ask what you can do for your country." In today's climate, that kind of selfless mindset could go a long way toward healing many of our societal wounds.

And in the church, Christ's example of love calls us to ask questions like these:

- How can I bless my family of faith this week?
- What can I do to encourage someone today?
- How can I show love to and through my church right now?

So much of life is lived with a "what's in it for me?" mentality. But Christ's example turns that question on its head. He calls us to give, not to grasp; to serve, not to seek status; to offer ourselves, not just our opinions

---

[75] G26, *Agapē* (ἀγάπη): "love, benevolence, goodwill." Unlike *philia* (friendship love) or *eros* (romantic desire), *agapē* describes God's self-giving love, revealed most fully in Christ's sacrifice.

[76] Peter Thomas O'Brien, *The Letter to the Ephesians*, The Pillar New Testament Commentary (Grand Rapids, MI: W.B. Eerdmans Publishing Co., 1999), 354.

or our leftovers, in loving sacrifice for the good of others. This is what it means to walk in love.

Holy Living

Maturing in Christ leads to holy living. Growing into the image of our heavenly Father means learning to love what God loves and turning our backs on everything that displeases Him. That's where Paul goes next. He warns believers not to fall for the world's distorted view of sexuality.

Like Paul's first-century audience, we live in a sex-saturated culture. For a long time, sexuality was treated as something dark, embarrassing, or shameful, a topic to be avoided. But that's not a biblical view either. Scripture presents human sexuality as something beautiful and God-ordained when lived out in the right context.

Fast-forward to today, and we've overcorrected into a cultural free-for-all. "Anything goes" has become the norm, and "if it feels good, do it" is the gospel of the day. Sex is everywhere.

In Paul's world, casual sex, orgies, and even religious prostitution were rampant cultural norms, especially in Ephesus, home to the Temple of Artemis, one of the seven wonders of the ancient world and a center of sexualized pagan worship.

In a world where even Christians can get confused about what love is and what holiness looks like, Paul draws a sharp contrast between the self-giving love of

Christ and the self-serving counterfeit of worldly passion. For Paul, nothing could be further from the love Christ modeled than sexual relationships outside God's design.[77]

N.T. Wright offers a sobering perspective on casual sex, describing it as a parody of true intimacy, like drinking from a muddy stream when fresh water is nearby or listening to a damaged recording while a live symphony plays next door. What our culture often celebrates as thrilling or liberating, Wright exposes as ultimately empty and harmful.[78]

The emotional buzz of an illicit relationship may feel intoxicating, but, like a drug, it leaves people numb, disappointed, and spiritually depleted. He reminds us that our bodies speak a language of total belonging in sexual union, and when that belonging is absent, we are living a lie. Eventually, that lie unravels, and with it, hearts and relationships unravel.[79]

Wright also insists that God's wrath is not arbitrary punishment but the built-in consequence of living out of sync with God's design. Sexual immorality doesn't just jeopardize our future inheritance; it cuts us off from participating in the life of God's kingdom even now.[80]

---

[77] Sproul, *Purpose of God*, 122–23.
[78] Wright, *Paul for Everyone*, 56–64.
[79] Wright, *Paul for Everyone*, 57–60.
[80] Wright, *Paul for Everyone*, 62–63.

These are hard words. They weren't popular in Paul's day, and they aren't popular now. But Paul wasn't aiming for popularity. He was pointing us to the kingdom of God.

Spiritual Practice: A Daily Dress Rehearsal

Each morning this week, begin your day with a sixty-second prayer:

> *Father, I want to grow into Your image today. Clothe me with Your love. Wrap me in Your holiness. Fill me with Your Spirit. May my life fit the life of Christ a little more today than it did yesterday. Amen.*

Try pairing this prayer with the simple act of getting dressed. As you button a shirt or tie your shoes, let it become a tangible reminder of what it means to "put on the new self" in Christ (Ephesians 4:24 ESV). Allow this daily rhythm to be a dress rehearsal for growing into God's love and holiness throughout the day.

Living in the Spirit's Light

In all of this, Paul is challenging these churches, and now us, to live in a way that shows the world what God's design for human life truly is. He's calling us to live in Christ's resurrection power, as God lights our path through His Word.[81] That kind of light-filled resurrection life brings renewal.

---

[81] J. B. Bond, "The Epistle of Paul the Apostle to the Ephesians," in *The Grace New Testament Commentary*, ed. Robert N. Wilkin (Denton, TX: Grace Evangelical Society, 2010), 883.

In our ministry, we've seen this promised transformation take root in real lives. We've watched young people reject promiscuity to honor God and preserve intimacy for a future spouse. We've walked alongside friends breaking free from the grip of pornography. Others have turned away from extramarital affairs and found restoration through repentance and grace. Some have been delivered from worldly identities and unholy desires that once defined them and are now walking in committed, God-honoring relationships, rooted in truth, shaped by love, and sustained by the Spirit.

I love how *The Message* paraphrases verse 14, probably a line from an early Christian hymn, against the backdrop of this sexual confusion and spiritual sleepwalking:

Wake up from your sleep,

Climb out of your coffins;

Christ will show you the light![82]

Paul reminds us that once we lived in darkness. More than that, we were part of the darkness. Now, he says, "you are light in the Lord" (Eph. 5:8 ESV). That's a bold claim. He doesn't just say we carry light or follow it; he says we *are* light.[83]

---

[82] Eugene H. Peterson, *The Message: The Bible in Contemporary Language*, Eph 5:14.

[83] G5457, *Phōs* (φῶς): light, radiance, or illumination. Paul says believers *are* light in the Lord, not merely carriers of light.

What does it mean to live as children of light? It means shining honesty into hidden corners of our lives. It means cultivating goodness and truth even when no one else is watching. It means being the kind of people whose presence brings clarity, not confusion. It means being people of hope rather than cynicism.

Sometimes our light feels dim. Sometimes it flickers. But as we walk in the Spirit and absorb the truths of God's Word, our lives begin to glow with His glory. It's not flashy or loud; it's just steady, trustworthy light, like a candle in a dark room. Light doesn't have to argue with darkness. It simply shows up, and darkness scatters.

In a world lulled to sleep by immorality, greed, and self-indulgence, Paul says that it's time to wake up. It's time to mature into the kind of example we are called to be, not by finger-pointing or condemnation but by living the kind of lives, building the kind of marriages, and nurturing the kind of families that shine God's light into a broken world.

In Ephesus, one of the gods widely worshiped was associated with wine and drunken revelry. To commune with this so-called deity and receive guidance, worshipers believed they had to be drunk. Intoxication was the gateway to hearing and obeying their god.[84] That is not too different from our own time.

---

[84] Anders, *Galatians, Ephesians, Philippians, Colossians*, 172.

Today, many still turn to substances to escape or to find meaning. Some are trapped in cycles of addiction that wound not only their own lives but also those of their families, cycles passed down through generations. It is heartbreaking to watch once-respected members of a community spiral into brokenness and despair by losing control through substance abuse.

Into that kind of brokenness, Paul speaks a better word:

> "Do not get drunk with wine, for that is debauchery, but be filled with the Spirit, addressing one another in psalms and hymns and spiritual songs, singing and making melody to the Lord with your heart, giving thanks always and for everything to God the Father in the name of our Lord Jesus Christ, submitting to one another out of reverence for Christ." (Ephesians 5:18–21 ESV)

Instead of letting our lives be controlled by substances, we are to live under the influence of the Holy Spirit.[85] Our relationships, once marked by chaos and division, are to be filled with worship, gratitude, and willing submission. As we "make melody to the Lord" from the heart, we become part of a new kind of community, shaped by grace and strengthened through worshipful fellowship. As we grow in this new

---

[85] G4151, *Pneuma* (πνεῦμα): Spirit, breath, or wind. It is used throughout the New Testament for the Holy Spirit, the personal divine presence empowering and sustaining God's people.

community, we learn to submit to one another out of reverence for Christ, putting the good of our families and the good of our family of faith ahead of our own.

That last phrase, "submitting to one another," is the hinge for everything that follows. The Greek word translated "submit" is a military term meaning "to arrange under," "to place oneself beneath in order," or "to yield voluntarily." In the lines that follow, Paul will bring this concept home. Submission shaped by the Spirit begins in our closest relationships. He uses the idea of submission here not to enforce hierarchy but to call believers into a Spirit-shaped posture of humility and mutual care. Paul paints a picture of Spirit-filled families, in which every relationship is shaped by our reverence for Christ and a desire to reflect His love (a concept that will be further discussed in chapter 8).

Being "filled with the Spirit" isn't a one-time emotional high or dramatic event.[86] It's a posture of openness, a daily willingness to be influenced and empowered by God's presence. Paul contrasts it with drunkenness not only because both affect behavior but also because both determine what or who controls us. Max Turner points out that Paul's contrast emphasizes "the controlling influence upon the believer's life,"

---

[86] G4137. *Plēroō* (πληρόω): to fill or make complete. In Ephesians 5:18, the verb points to an ongoing action of being filled or continually influenced by the Spirit.

whether by intoxicating substances or by the Spirit's presence.[87]

The Spirit's filling isn't something we manufacture. It is something we receive, like breath or light. And the Spirit is revealed not just in extraordinary experiences but in the everyday beauty of community life: in the way we speak to each other, in the songs we sing, in the thankfulness we express, and in the humility with which we relate.

If we want to grow into the Father's wardrobe, we must let the Spirit clothe us daily.

- Worship becomes the fitting room where our hearts are realigned.
- Gratitude becomes the thread that stitches humility into our habits.
- Submission becomes the daily rhythm of Christlike community.

Ephesians has been building toward this powerful call: *Be imitators of God.* It's a daunting command. If it doesn't humble us, we may not be paying attention. We feel like children copying their older siblings, teenagers trying on their dad's sport coat, or toddlers swimming in a T-shirt five sizes too big.

---

[87]Max Turner, "Ephesians," in *New Bible Commentary: 21st Century Edition*, eds. D. A. Carson, R.T. France, J.A. Motyer, and Gordon J. Wenham, 4th ed. (Downers Grove, IL: InterVarsity Press, 1994), 1242.

That's where Paul finds us, but it's not where he wants to leave us. Through worshipful fellowship, holy living, and sacrificial love, we begin to grow up in Christ. Bit by bit, grace by grace, we start to fit into the wardrobe God has given us. We grow into our Father's clothes. And as we do, we become a witness to the world, a living picture of the God who is shaping us in His image.

In this chapter, we've explored Paul's invitation to grow into the likeness of our heavenly Father. We've taken off the grave clothes of sin and selfishness and stepped into a resurrection wardrobe stitched with love, holiness, and Spirit-filled worship. This isn't instant. It's the daily work of grace, practiced in community. But as we imitate God, step by faithful step, the clothes begin to fit.

Praying the Message

Lord God, You've called us to walk in love and live as children of light. Help us to reflect Your holiness in a world that often confuses darkness for truth. Teach us to live wisely, to love sacrificially, and to speak with grace. Guard our hearts from compromise, fill us with thanksgiving, and shape us so that our lives point to You. In Jesus's name, Amen.

Further Reflection

Ephesians 5:1-21

1. **Context Connection**
   It's natural for children to imitate their parents. I remember pretending to shave like my dad, wearing his sport coat that swallowed me whole, and eventually growing into his shirts. Paul invites us to do the same with our heavenly Father, imitating His character until, step by step, the clothes of love, holiness, and Spirit-filled worship begin to fit.

   - Do you have special memories of imitating your parents or a parental figure?
   - What do you think Paul means when he calls us to be "imitators of God"?

2. **Key Themes in the Text**
   Jesus is our ultimate example of love that is sacrificial, holy, and offered for the good of others.

   - Who does Paul cite as our example in practicing God's love?
   - What are some defining marks of this kind of love in everyday life?

3. **Church and Community Application**
   Paul calls believers to live holy lives, even in a culture saturated with immorality, and to practice worship that lifts hearts toward God in psalms, hymns, and spiritual songs.

- How do Paul's words about holiness in a context of rampant sexual immorality speak to our world today?
- What can this passage teach us about cultivating worship that is both diverse and Spirit-filled in the church?

4. **Personal Transformation**
   The call to imitate God touches every part of life: our words, choices, relationships, and acts of worship.
   - In what specific area of your life is God inviting you to "grow into His clothes" right now?
   - How might practicing love, holiness, or Spirit-led worship change the way you interact with others this week?
5. **Closing Blessing or Prayer Prompt**
   Lord, help me to walk in Your love, to pursue holiness, and to worship with a heart full of gratitude, so that I may grow daily into Your likeness.

Chapter 8

Homes and Workplaces Directed by the Spirit of God Ephesians 5:17–6:10

…submitting to one another out of reverence for Christ.
(Ephesians 5:21)

Walk through the doorway of any home, and you quickly sense what fills it. Some homes feel heavy, as though every word is weighed down with tension. Others overflow with warmth, laughter, and encouragement. What fills us eventually fills our households. Paul reminds us in Ephesians 5 that the difference lies in what controls our lives. "Do not get drunk with wine," he warns, "but be filled with the Spirit" (5:18).

This opening section serves as a bridge, connecting what has come before with what is about to follow. Paul shows us what a Spirit-led life looks like through a series of Greek participles: addressing (Eph. 5:19), singing and making melody (5:19), giving thanks (5:20), and submitting (5:21). These are the marks of a life under the Spirit's guiding influence.

When we are filled with the Holy Spirit, that filling changes the way we speak; we address one another with psalms, hymns, and spiritual songs (Eph. 5:19). It transforms the way we sing; we make melody to the Lord from our hearts (5:19). It reshapes the way we view life; we give thanks always and for everything to God the Father in the name of our Lord Jesus Christ (5:20). Most importantly, it redefines how we relate within the family of faith: we submit to one another out of reverence for Christ (5:21).[88]

Earlier, Paul warned us not to be drunk with wine, knowing its damaging effects. Instead, he urges us to drink deeply from the well of God's Spirit, for this filling produces clarity, gratitude, joy, and harmony. When the Holy Spirit leads our lives, He profoundly shapes the foundational relationships at the core of our homes.

In the first-century Roman world, households typically included husbands and wives, parents and children, and slaves and masters. Paul explains how faith in Christ reshapes these closest relationships. He shows the believers in and around Ephesus, and us

---

[88] G5293, *Hypotassō* (ὑποτάσσω): to place under, subordinate; in the middle voice it means to subject oneself or obey. It is often used in military contexts for arranging troops under a leader's command, but in the New Testament frequently describes voluntary yielding in relationships out of reverence for Christ.

today, what it looks like to get the church inside of us, beginning right at home.

Understanding the Cultural Context

Many modern readers cringe when they encounter this part of Paul's letter, and I understand why. For generations, this passage and similar passages have been misused to portray Paul as misogynistic or racist and to justify oppressive systems that devalue women or condone slavery. Yet much of that reaction comes from a failure to consider the historical and cultural context in which Paul lived and wrote.

The first-century Roman world was deeply patriarchal. Women and children were often treated as little more than property. Slavery was so embedded in society that imagining life without it would have been as unthinkable to Paul as imagining life without the internet is to my kids today. When we take that context into account, we begin to see just how remarkable Paul's teaching really was.

In a world that saw women as inferior, Paul called Christian husbands to love their wives with the same self-giving love Christ showed on the cross. In a culture where children had few rights and were expected to remain silent, he challenged parents to raise them not with harshness but with grace, discipline, and loving instruction. In a society that viewed slaves as soulless tools, Paul affirmed their worth as human beings created in God's image—people for whom Christ died. He even commanded Christian masters to treat their slaves with dignity, respect, and fairness. These were radical instructions in a world that barely recognized slaves' humanity.

While Paul did not call for the immediate dismantling of slavery, his words planted gospel seeds that would one day break the system apart. When he told masters to stop threatening their slaves and reminded them that they too had a Master in heaven, Paul undermined the very foundation of hierarchy and control. His teaching echoed the radical truth of Galatians 3:28—that in Christ there is "neither slave nor free."

Far from reinforcing cultural hierarchies, Paul's vision for the Christian household elevated women, children, and slaves in ways that honored their God-given dignity and pointed toward a more just and Spirit-shaped way of life.

Lives of God-Honoring Submission

Bringing our lives under the controlling influence of God's Spirit means learning to live out our faith within our homes. According to Paul, that begins with submission. The word "submission" carries the sense of willingly yielding one's own rights or will out of reverence for Christ. When shaped by the spirit of sacrifice, it reflects the pattern God designed for all relationships, a humble, Christlike posture that protects authority from becoming abusive and protects power from overshadowing love.[89] "Submitting to one another out of reverence for Christ" (Eph. 5:21) is not a mere tagline; it is the foundation of Spirit-shaped relationships. This principle applies in the home, the workplace, and the church.

In each of these settings, those with authority are called to lead with humility, placing others' needs before their own. Those under authority are called to respond with respect and honor.[90] When each person operates with the good of the other in mind, the whole system works beautifully.

In ministry settings, I am often asked questions like, "Who has the authority to make this decision?" or "What role gives someone the right to lead in this area?" People are usually seeking a clear hierarchy, a kind of flowchart of rights, privileges, and responsibilities. Most of the time, you can find those answers in a church's bylaws, but, ideally, you should not have to resort to that. Here is what I have learned: If you must assert formal authority, you probably do not have much of it. That's true in our churches and in our homes and workplaces.

Wives and Husbands: Spirit-Shaped Marriage

Paul begins with the marriage relationship, showing how the Holy Spirit's presence reshapes the most intimate bond in the home. Wives are called to respect

---

[89] Adapted from Rasnake, *Ephesians*, 78.

[90] Anders, *Galatians, Ephesians, Philippians, Colossians*, 173.

and honor their husbands "as to the Lord" (Eph. 5:22). This is not blind obedience, nor is it a loss of identity. It is a posture of willing respect that reflects trust in Christ.

Husbands, meanwhile, are called to an even weightier task: to love their wives "as Christ loved the church and gave himself up for her" (Eph. 5:25). In the first-century world, husbands often ruled their households with authority and privilege. Paul turns that assumption about how things ought to be on its head. He calls Christian husbands to lead not with control but with sacrifice, not with demands but with devotion.

The love Paul describes is self-giving, cruciform love. It is love that seeks the flourishing of the other even at great personal cost. As Timothy Keller observes, "The Christian teaching does not offer a choice between fulfillment and sacrifice but rather says that you will never find fulfillment unless you are willing to surrender yourself continually in many small ways."[91] Marriage is not about one spouse winning and the other losing. It is about both surrendering to Christ, and, in turn, surrendering to one another in love.

When husbands and wives live this way, marriage becomes more than a social contract or legal arrangement. It becomes a living parable of Christ's love for His church. The world sees in Christian

---

[91] Timothy Keller, *The Meaning of Marriage: Facing the Complexities of Commitment with the Wisdom of God* (New York: Dutton, 2011), 47.

marriage a reflection of the gospel itself: two becoming one, not through grasping for control but through Spirit-shaped submission and love.

Parents and Children: Spirit-Shaped Parenting

After speaking to husbands and wives, Paul turns to the relationship between parents and children. He begins with a simple but profound command: "Children, obey your parents in the Lord, for this is right" (Ephesians 6:1). Obedience to parents is not only practical but also rooted in God's design for family life. Paul anchors it in the Ten Commandments: "Honor your father and mother" (Eph. 6:2). This is the first commandment with a promise attached: "that it may go well with you and that you may live long in the land" (Eph. 6:3).

For children, obedience and honor are expressions of their faith in the Lord. Respect for parents is one of the earliest ways a child learns to live under God's authority. Honoring parents is more than blind compliance; it is the shaping of character through trust, respect, and gratitude.

Paul then speaks directly to fathers, though his words apply to all parents: "Do not provoke your children to anger, but bring them up in the discipline and instruction of the Lord" (Ephesians 6:4). In Paul's world, fathers held enormous power, including the legal right to control or even disown their children. Against that backdrop, Paul calls parents not to harshness but to nurturing, not to provoke but to guide. Discipline is not about punishment; it is about forming the heart and character of children in the ways of the Lord. Instruction is not about controlling their future; it is about passing on faith, wisdom, and love.

Paul uses the word *ektrephō* when he urges fathers to "bring up" their children in the training and instruction of the Lord (Eph. 6:4).[92] The term means "to nourish, to feed, to cherish into maturity," the way one carefully tends a life so that it flourishes. Spirit-led parenting is not about domination or neglect but about cultivating growth through guidance, patience, and love.

True growth, as Larry Crabb reminds us, begins with honesty: "We can't grow until we are willing to face the truth about ourselves."[93] Spirit-shaped parenting, then, holds together both truth and tenderness. Parents are called to lead with consistency and strength but also with compassion and encouragement. Children are called to respond with honor and trust.

Together, these relationships form the heart of the home, where the love of Christ can be seen, practiced, and passed on to the next generation. As Tim Kimmel wisely puts it, "The primary job of parents is not to

---

[92] G1625, *Ektrephō* (ἐκτρέφω): to nourish, bring up, rear, or cherish. Paul uses it to express Christ's ongoing tender provision for His church and to describe a father's responsibility not just to feed but to nurture children toward maturity in Christ.

[93] Larry Crabb, *Inside Out* (Colorado Springs: NavPress, 1988), 28.

raise successful children, but to raise children who know how to give and receive God's grace."[94]

That kind of grace begins with humility. Spirit-led homes are not built on appearances, but on confession, forgiveness, and confidence that love does not vanish when we fail. When parents own their weaknesses and children learn that grace covers imperfection, the home itself becomes a living picture of God's faithful love.

Holy Rhythms

Spirit-shaped parenting doesn't stop at words of guidance; it is reinforced by the rhythms of daily life. When we bring our homes under the direction of God's Spirit and relate to one another through Christlike actions of sacrifice, words like *respect*, *love*, *devotion*, *obedience*, *honor*, *consideration*, *fairness*, and *service* begin to define our lives. Lives of submission and sacrifice flourish without the weight of oppressive hierarchy, setting us free to live God's story of love, grace, mercy, and joy.

One of the ways we relinquish control and submit to the Spirit's leading in our home is through shared spiritual rhythms. We pray together with the children on the way to school. It's amazing to hear each family member pray for the others and whatever else is on that person's heart. These honest moments are sacred and often the best part of my day. We hold hands and pray

---

[94] Tim Kimmel, *Grace-Based Parenting: Set Your Family Free* (Nashville, TN: Thomas Nelson, 2005), 52.

before meals. We worship together as a family. These are not flashy events. They are simply real moments where we pause and remember who we are before God.

We've never done any of this perfectly, and some seasons are more consistent than others. But those small, sacred pauses have helped keep our home oriented toward grace. Spirit-led homes aren't marked by perfection. They're marked by an openness to God in the everyday details.

While these intentional rhythms keep our home oriented toward grace, it is often in the ordinary, unscripted moments that God-honoring submission takes its deepest root.

Everyday Submission and Sacrifice: Levity and Grace

In our family, we've discovered that submission and sacrifice do not just show up in big defining moments. They thrive in the everyday language of our home, in small phrases that keep us honest, humble, and connected.

Over the years, a few sayings have become like mantras in our marriage and parenting:

- **"Almost every day."** Lisa and I often say that we have a happy marriage, *almost every day*. After nearly three decades together, still being able to say that feels like a solid accomplishment. We also like to think we're good parents, *almost every day.* I hope our kids would agree. Some days we get it right. Other days, we don't. The key is staying on the path. Even when we stumble, we are still heading in the right direction, *almost every day.*

- **"I have other positive qualities."** This one usually surfaces after someone messes something up. The offender will shrug, grin, and say, *"Well, I have other positive qualities."* It is our tongue-in-cheek way of admitting imperfection without collapsing into shame. Just as often, someone else in the family will say, *"well, you have other positive qualities,"* to lift up a sibling or parent who is being too hard on themselves. It is a small but powerful way of taking responsibility while also affirming that perfection is not a requirement for being deeply loved.
- **"That was not my shining moment."** This is how we name a poor choice or a less-than-stellar reaction. If I forgot to roll the dumpster to the curb, *that was not my shining moment.* If I lose my temper, I will say the same thing. It is not an excuse; it is a step toward humility and often the doorway to an apology.

I don't know if these phrases would work in your home, but, for us, they create a culture of honesty, levity, and grace. They remind us that we are on the same team. And I think that is something like what Paul had in mind when he called us to submit "to one another out of reverence to Christ." Spirit-led relationships are rooted in grace, humility, and love, *almost every day.*

Submission and sacrifice are lived out in our homes in these small everyday acts of grace. But these ideas only take root if the people sharing them are, emotionally and spiritually, healthy enough to offer and receive them. God-honoring submission thrives not only in how we treat each other but also in how we care for ourselves.

Caring for Yourself as an Act of Preparation for Submission

I've often heard it said that there are two kinds of people in the world: those who are seeing a good professional counselor and those who should be seeing a good professional counselor. From experience, I can tell you that if you are struggling to cope with life's challenges, seeing a wise counselor can be a tremendous gift, not only for yourself but also for the people who love you most.

Practicing the art of submitting to one another is not only about how we treat other people. It is also about how we steward ourselves. When we care for our physical, mental, and spiritual health, we can offer our families the best version of who we are. Neglecting those areas eventually diminishes what we can give at home, in the church, and in the workplace. As Henry Cloud reminds us, "We are responsible to others, not for others. Healthy boundaries make genuine love possible."[95]

In that sense, self-care becomes an act of love. Choosing counseling, exercise, prayer, rest, or healthy rhythms is not indulgence. It is preparation for service. When we submit to Christ's Spirit in these ways, we position ourselves to show up with strength and grace for the people who depend on us most.

This same principle extends beyond the walls of our homes. Just as caring for ourselves allows us to love our families well, submitting to Christ in our work allows us to serve faithfully in our jobs.

A Radically Countercultural Instruction

In Paul's world, husbands wielded unchecked authority. Yet Paul flips the script. He does not tell men to control their wives. He tells them to die for them, not necessarily in a literal sense but in daily acts of dying to self: listening, serving, sacrificing, and choosing grace over pride and presence over power.

This kind of love is not weak. It is holy. Christ's love purifies, lifts, restores, and cherishes. Paul's language of "washing with the word" and "presenting her without blemish" is priestly, not patriarchal. It is about drawing someone into that person's fullness, not keeping that person under your thumb.

---

[95] Henry Cloud and John Townsend, *Boundaries: When to Say Yes, How to Say No to Take Control of Your Life* (Grand Rapids, MI: Zondervan, 1992), 31.

The same principle carries into Paul's vision of parenting. In a culture where fathers often ruled with severity, Paul calls them instead to *nourish* their children, to bring them up in the Lord's training and instruction with patience and tenderness. Spirit-led authority is never about domination. It is about laying yourself down for the sake of another's flourishing.

Spirit-shaped submission and sacrifice do not stop at the front door of our homes; they walk with us into the workplace.

Spiritual Practice: Daily Submission

Submission and sacrifice mark the Spirit-shaped atmosphere of the Christian household that must be learned in practice, not only in big decisions but in daily moments of humility, love, and surrender. This rhythm does not happen automatically. It begins when we ask the Spirit to move in us, inviting Him to shape our responses before the day even begins.

One practical way to do this is to begin each morning with a simple, intentional prayer:

> *Lord, fill me with Your Spirit today. Let my words, attitudes, and actions reflect Your love. Teach me to honor others, to listen before I speak, and to serve instead of demand. May I submit my desires to You and my preferences to those I love for Your glory. For Jesus's sake and in His name, Amen.*

Equally important is ending the day with reflection. As we review the conversations, decisions, and interactions that shaped our hours, we can ask

- Where did I model Christ's love today?
- Where did I insist on my own way?
- Where do I need grace and growth for tomorrow?

In this pattern of morning surrender and evening reflection, we open ourselves to the Spirit's transforming work. The discipline of practicing such regular self-examination is important because the Christian faith is not confined to Sunday worship; it forms every part of life.

Being Christlike in Our Workplaces

Paul's words to slaves and masters, while written in a different cultural context, offer powerful principles that still apply today. In the Roman world, slavery was a widespread economic system that often resembled what we might call indentured servitude more than the racialized slavery familiar from modern history. Still, it was an institution marked by deep inequality, often leaving people vulnerable to exploitation. While Paul did not endorse slavery, he planted the seeds of its undoing by urging believers to see themselves and others as servants of Christ, equal before God and accountable to Him. These same truths speak powerfully into the relationships between employees and employers today, where the call to mutual respect, integrity, and grace remains urgently needed.[96]

Over time, submission and sacrifice become more than theological concepts. They become the quiet current that carries us toward deeper relationships, stronger homes, and a more faithful witness to the world. And this witness leads us to serve faithfully in our workplaces.

Paul's words to slaves and masters, while written in a different cultural context, offer powerful principles that still apply today. In our time, these truths speak into the relationships between employees and employers, and they are needed now more than ever.

Growing up on a family farm gave me a certain kind of work ethic from an early age. Some chores were expected simply because we lived rent-free in the house. Other jobs, like driving a tractor, hoeing cotton, mending fences, or hauling hay, came with compensation. My grandfather and my dad, both of whom I respected deeply, could also be tough taskmasters. They didn't hand out praise easily, but they taught me how to work hard and how to take correction when I missed the mark.

---

96 See Mark D. Roberts, *Ephesians*, The Story of God Bible Commentary, ed. Scot McKnight (Grand Rapids, MI: Zondervan, 2016), 296–300; Wright, *Paul for Everyone*, 163–5; and Craig S. Keener, *The IVP Bible Background Commentary: New Testament* (Downers Grove, IL: InterVarsity Press, 1993), 552–53.

When I left home, I assumed that everyone had grown up like that—knowing how to work hard and give their best. But I quickly learned that wasn't the case. During college, I served as a youth pastor and worked a second job at a pet store chain. That retail experience opened my eyes. Smoke breaks were frequent, petty theft was common, people wasted time, and many did the bare minimum. I was surprised when the company began offering me management opportunities after just a short time on the job. At first, I was proud until I realized how low the bar was set. Just showing up on time and doing my job somewhat efficiently made me stand out.

I also noticed how poorly the company treated the few employees who did rise into management. As people were promoted from hourly to salaried positions, they were expected to work significantly more hours for less pay per hour when the math was done. It was clear that the system wasn't working well for the people at the bottom or the ones climbing to the top.

My own work experiences reminded me how much workplace relationships can either honor or diminish people. That is why Paul's words to slaves and masters still speak so powerfully into our employer-employee dynamics today. Into a world marked by wide chasms between managers and workers, Paul injects this transformative truth: a living relationship with King

Jesus impacts how we treat each other, wherever we are, whatever we do.

To the employee who feels unseen and unvalued and uses that frustration to justify clocking in late, scrolling social media on the clock, or cutting corners, Paul says, "Remember who your true Boss is." What kind of difference might it make if more of us viewed our daily tasks as opportunities to worship God by giving our very best?

As Dr. Martin Luther King Jr. once put it, if a person is called to be a street sweeper, he should sweep streets as faithfully as Michelangelo painted or Beethoven composed music. He should do his work so well that heaven and earth pause to say, "Here lived a great street sweeper who did his job well."[97] That kind of faithfulness, whether seen or unseen, reflects the kingdom of God. Even if no one else notices, God does. And Paul reminds us that God Himself will reward that kind of Spirit-led work.

To the Christian employer, Paul gives another challenge: Treat those under your supervision with dignity and grace. What would it look like if more Christian business owners and managers saw success not just in terms of profit but in terms of how well they cared for their people? What if employers began to view every employee as someone who bears the image of God and is loved by Christ? Even if such kindness

---

97 King, *Strength to Love*, 143.

and fairness go unnoticed in this world, Paul assures us that God honors those who walk the Jesus way, particularly because of how they lead and care for others.

He ends with a stinger: "There is no partiality with Him." It's a warning. It's a comfort. It's a line that levels every playing field. In a culture defined by status and power, Paul reminds us that we all kneel before the same Lord. The cross levels us. The Spirit unites us. Earthly roles may differ, but eternal worth is equal.

This challenges any modern Christian who would justify prejudice, power abuse, or favoritism. If God shows no partiality, neither should we. Christians should be beacons of fairness and grace in our homes, churches, and workplaces.

This section of Paul's letter reveals how the balance between the doctrine we believe and the way we live plays out in real, practical terms. If we call ourselves Christians, we are declaring that we follow King Jesus and carry His teachings wherever we go. Nowhere should that be more evident than in how we treat our spouses, our children, our parents, our coworkers, our employees, and our employers.

- Are we living lives marked by submission and sacrifice?
- When we consider our families, our churches, and our workplaces, do we spend more time

> thinking about what we are owed or what we can give?

At the cross, Jesus gave us the ultimate example of living in God's love. If we are going to build homes and workplaces directed by God's Spirit, we must follow that example. When we do, Jesus's story comes alive, not just in our beliefs but in our daily lives, in our jobs, and in the grace, truth, and kindness we show to one another.

Since these truths touch every part of life, including home, family, and work, it is only fitting that we turn them into prayer.

Praying the Message

Gracious Father, thank You for the gift of family and the calling to reflect Christ in our homes. Teach us to submit to one another in love, to serve with humility, and to lead with grace. Fill our households with Your Spirit. Shape our relationships with patience, kindness, and respect. May our homes be places where Christ is honored and His love is lived. In Jesus's name, Amen.

Further Reflection

Ephesians 5:17–6:10

1. **Context Connection**
   Paul contrasts being filled with wine, which leads to foolishness, with being filled with the Spirit, which leads to worship, gratitude, and transformed relationships. Spirit-filled living changes the atmosphere of our homes, our workplaces, and our communities.

   - How does Paul describe the difference between being under the influence of wine and being under the influence of the Spirit?
   - How does this passage connect Spirit-filled living with the way we treat others in our closest relationships?

2. **Key Themes in the Text**
   "Submitting to one another out of reverence to Christ" is the guiding principle for Spirit-directed households. In Paul's world, this played out between husbands and wives, parents and children, and masters and slaves. In our world, it applies to marriages, families, and workplace relationships.

   - What kind of relationship does Paul describe between husbands and wives? Between parents and children?

- How does the idea of willing submission challenge cultural ideas about power and authority?

3. **Church and Community Application**
   This passage has been misread at times to justify control or abuse. Read carefully, it paints a picture of love, sacrifice, respect, honor, and sincerity flowing out of Spirit-filled submission to Christ.

   - What are some ways this passage has been misused in church history or in homes?
   - How can we teach and live it in a way that reflects the gospel's call to love and serve one another?

4. **Personal Transformation**
   As we submit ourselves to King Jesus, the Spirit reshapes our relationships from the inside out.

   - What changes might happen in your marriage, family, or workplace if you applied Paul's instructions more fully?
   - Where might you need to release control and ask the Spirit to lead you into humility and service?

5. **Closing Blessing or Prayer Prompt**
   Lord, fill me with Your Spirit so that my words, actions, and relationships reflect Your love. Help me submit to others as I submit to You and let my home and work honor Christ in every way.

CHAPTER 9

GEARING UP FOR SPIRITUAL WARFARE EPHESIANS 6:10–17

Finally, be strong in the Lord and in the strength of his might. Put on the whole armor of God, that you may be able to stand against the schemes of the devil. For we do not wrestle against flesh and blood, but against the rulers, against the authorities, against the cosmic powers over this present darkness, against the spiritual forces of evil in the heavenly places.
(Ephesians 6:10-12)

Most battles do not make the headlines. Some are fought in quiet living rooms where a marriage teeters on the edge. Others take place in hospital rooms where fear whispers in the night. Still others unfold in workplaces where integrity is tested and in churches where seeds of division are sown. Behind all of them is a conflict we cannot see with our eyes but one that is real nonetheless.

Every firefighter knows you do not enter a burning building without gear. Every law enforcement officer knows you do not step into danger without the right equipment. Every soldier knows you do not march onto the battlefield without armor. The stakes are too high to go in unprepared.

Paul understood this reality in a deeper way. When he wrote to the churches, he was under house arrest in Rome, chained to a soldier, and awaiting trial for preaching Christ. No longer free to travel or speak face-to-face with the congregations he loved, Paul picked up his pen to encourage them amid their own unseen battles.

This letter to the Ephesians paints a sweeping picture of God's barrier-breaking, grace-filled salvation story. All kinds of people, regardless of background, are welcomed into the household of God through Jesus Christ. Yet Paul does not end his letter with lofty words about identity or unity alone. He reminds us that all these truths are lived out in a battle. The blessings of God's grace, the calls to holiness and love, and the summons to unity and faithfulness—they are all worked out in the middle of conflict.

So, Paul closes his letter with an exhortation. Gear up, be prepared, and stand firm because the Christian life is not a playground. It is a battleground.

Getting It Wrong in Different Ways

When it comes to spiritual warfare, Christians often drift into one of two unhealthy extremes before discovering the balanced way Paul describes.

Some treat the Christian life as if it were only about personal inspiration, moral living, or church attendance. The devil becomes nothing more than a cartoon figure with a pitchfork, and evil is reduced to human mistakes or broken social systems. As the poet Charles Baudelaire once observed, "The devil's first trick is to convince us that he doesn't exist."[98] Many people today have fallen prey to that trick. When we ignore the battle, we lose sight of the very real enemy who "prowls around like a roaring lion, seeking someone to devour" (1 Pet. 5:8). By pretending the struggle is not real, we make ourselves easy prey.

Others take the opposite approach. Every flat tire, missed opportunity, or difficult day is credited to direct demonic attack. Fear replaces trust, and spiritual life becomes dominated by suspicion and paranoia. When everything is blamed on the devil, the focus shifts from the victory of Christ to the activity of the enemy. This approach leaves believers weary, anxious, and unbalanced.

Paul offers a different path. He does not deny the enemy's presence, nor does he encourage obsession

---

[98] Charles Baudelaire, *Paris Spleen, 1869,* trans. Louise Varèse (New York: New Directions, 1970), 52. Translation from *Le Spleen de Paris: Petits Poèmes en prose* (Paris, 1869), 53.

with him. Instead, he directs our attention to Christ. The command is clear: Be strong in the Lord and in the strength of his might. The call is not to muster up inner toughness or clever strategies. The strength comes from God alone. The armor belongs to God, not us. The battle is not ours to win but Christ's victory to stand upon.

N.T. Wright once admitted the difficulty of writing about spiritual warfare. As he worked on his Ephesians commentary, interruptions piled up, from unexpected home repairs to a computer crash that stopped his progress entirely.[99] Coincidence? Perhaps. But his experience mirrors the disruptions many believers face.

Distractions can come in the strangest forms—sometimes comical, sometimes shocking, but always pulling attention away from God's work. One deacon once told me about a revival service where the Spirit was moving powerfully, right up until a bat swooped through the rafters and everyone forgot the altar call. The Spirit didn't stop moving; the congregation just got distracted for a moment. The whole scene left a lasting impression. Dr. Vernon Davis recalled a funeral disrupted by a child who wandered in, opened the casket, and left the grieving congregation horrified, on top of being in the middle of a church conflict. Reflecting later, Davis said, "When things like that happen at the worst possible time, you just have to

---

[99] Wright, *Paul for Everyone*, 72.

shrug your shoulders and acknowledge that there just has to be a devil."[100]

I faced my own share of such disruption while drafting this book. Major spinal surgery and severe postoperative complications brought me, quite literally, to the brink of death. Yet through it all, my family and I were upheld by God's sustaining power. By His grace, the book was finished and published, and my prayer is that it will encourage others along the way.

These kinds of moments remind us that the Christian life is never lived on neutral ground. Paul understood this well, which is why he spoke so clearly about the reality of spiritual warfare and the need to stand firm in the Lord.

Paul will not allow us to take spiritual warfare lightly, nor will he let us stumble into either ditch of denial or obsession. Instead, he calls us to clarity, sobriety, and balance—to stand strong in the Lord against a very real enemy. And to keep us from mistaking who that enemy truly is, Paul reminds us exactly where the real battle lies.

Identifying Our True Enemy

At the heart of Paul's teaching on spiritual warfare is this: we need to remember who our true enemy is. In times of conflict, fear, and division, we have a dangerous tendency to misidentify the enemy, and

---

[100] Vernon Davis, class lecture, Logsdon Seminary, April 2001, author's personal notes.

when we get that wrong, everything else begins to unravel.

Too often, we start to see the people who disagree with us in church or the church across town as the problem. We adopt the combative, polarized language that dominates our culture and soon find ourselves surrounded by "enemies." Democrats become the threat. Republicans become the problem. Liberals are ruining everything. Conservatives are stuck in the past. We divide the world into tribes and echo chambers, defending "our side" without question and opposing "their side" without grace.

And while we are distracted by all that, the real enemy smiles.

Paul reminds us that our struggle is not against flesh and blood. It is not against people. It is against spiritual forces of evil—powers that seek to distort the truth, divide God's people, and derail the mission of Christ. When we aim our anger and frustration at other human beings, we end up wasting our energy fighting the wrong battle, and we leave ourselves vulnerable to the one who is truly working against us. When we try to fight a spiritual battle with resources of the flesh, we always fall short.

That is why Paul calls us to "stand against the devil's schemes" (Eph. 6:11). He knows the enemy is not obvious. If the devil showed up looking like a cartoon villain, with horns, a tail, and a pitchfork, we would know to run the other way. But the devil is far more subtle. He studies us. He knows the weak spots in our armor, and he leverages them with deceptive precision.[101]

Eugene Peterson once observed that the devil is a master of promoting evil that does not look like evil.[102] Sometimes it even looks like good. That kind of subtle deception is far more dangerous than the obvious sins we already know to avoid. It reminds me of a confession I once heard from a lay leader who had served under a prominent but morally compromised pastor. He said, "He could get you to do bad things before you realized you were doing bad things."

That is how deception works. It is subtle, slow, almost invisible. Of course, Paul has already warned us clearly in Ephesians 4–5 about obvious forms of sin: bitterness, slander, sexual immorality, and greed, among others. We still need those warnings, especially in a world that now celebrates many of those very things. But we also need the challenge to stand against the devil's tricks, because not all sin comes in the form of open rebellion. Sometimes it sneaks in wearing a disguise.

A healthy desire to provide for your family can become a soul-suffocating obsession with achievement and status. A conviction to stand for truth can curdle slowly into hatred for those who disagree with you, building the very walls Jesus came to tear down. A

---

101 A.T. Robertson, *Word Pictures in the New Testament*, Eph 6:11.

102 Peterson, *Practice Resurrection*, Kindle Page 2942.

passion for reaching the lost can be twisted into consumer-driven ministries or prosperity gospels where self-interest masquerades as spiritual growth. Spiritually unformed souls, craving energy without the cost of discipleship, gather in crowds, drawn by feel-good messages that promise blessing but rarely mention surrender or obedience.

The devil's schemes are not always dramatic. Often, they are disguised. Evil does not always look like evil. That is why Paul urges us to open our eyes, stay grounded in truth, recognize the real enemy, and prepare ourselves with the spiritual armor only God can provide. Without that armor, we will falter.

Once we recognize the enemy for who he is, the next question is how to respond to those who have been deceived by him. Scripture reminds us that our struggle is not against them, even when their actions or words oppose the gospel. Paul tells Timothy that the Lord's servant "must not be quarrelsome but must be kind to everyone, able to teach, not resentful. Opponents must be gently instructed, in the hope that God will grant them repentance leading them to a knowledge of the truth" (2 Tim. 2:24–25). In other words, those who resist us are not enemies to defeat but captives to rescue. Spiritual warfare is not about overpowering people but about participating in their redemption. We engage the real enemy through truth and prayer while showing compassion to those caught in his snare.

Paul's answer is simple but profound: stand firm.

Standing Firm

The devil is a cunning adversary, one who has been tripping up God's people since the Garden of Eden. How can we possibly stand against such a crafty foe, especially on a battlefield that feels so confusing? Paul does not offer a brand-new strategy. Instead, he calls us back to what he has been saying throughout the entire letter. In the face of spiritual opposition, Paul gives this timeless instruction: "Stand firm" (Eph. 6:13). In these few verses about spiritual warfare, Paul uses the word *stand* four times. It is not just repetition. It is emphasis. He is steadying us with these words.

Peterson captures the tone of this instruction well when he imagines Paul saying:

> *Steady now. Stand your ground. Stay on your feet. Don't let yourself get distracted. Don't check out every new offering or program that comes along. Stand firm in this place of blessing that we now inhabit. Stand firm in the church God has given us, this gift of a place and community where we have access to Scripture, to Jesus, and to companions in praise and suffering. This is a living word. Keep listening. Take your stand with these people.*[103]

When we first approach Paul's teaching on spiritual warfare, we might expect a grand battle plan, some offensive strategy for taking ground. But instead, Paul

---

[103] Peterson, *Practice Resurrection*, Kindle Page 2899–915.

gives a strikingly simple instruction: stay put and stand firm.

That is a needed word in today's consumer-driven church culture. It has become commonplace to hop from church to church, seeking out the next spiritual high, what we often call "being fed." But Paul's challenge is far more grounded. He calls us to remain steady. He challenges us to hold our ground in the real, often messy, imperfect church community where God is doing the long work of sanctifying us through obedience, service, and grace.

Standing firm does not always look dramatic. Sometimes it looks like showing up again. Often it looks like praying when we do not feel like it. It almost always looks like loving people who are hard to love. Standing firm means staying rooted in Scripture and in the body of Christ when it would be easier to drift away.

Paul's battle cry is not "Charge!" but "Stand!" It is not glamorous, but it is powerful. And it is exactly what we need.

So how do we stand firm in Christ's strength? Paul sketches a vivid picture using the very equipment of the soldier beside him.

Wearing the Right Armor

Paul wants us to be ready for the spiritual battle that rages around us. That means

- recognizing our true enemy,

- standing firm alongside our brothers and sisters in faith,
- and putting on the proper gear for the fight.

We can imagine Paul glancing at the Roman soldier chained to him as he writes, drawing out vivid instructions for how we are to equip ourselves.

The first piece of spiritual equipment is the belt of truth. Before a soldier put on his armor, he fastened a belt around his waist to hold everything in place. Paul begins here: "Stand therefore… having fastened on the belt of truth" (Eph. 6:14).[104] Just as the soldier's belt freed him to move unhindered, truth frees us from lies that choke the gospel. When we live truthfully with God, others, and ourselves, we can move forward in faith. Spiros Zodhiates points out that the Greek word for "truth" (*aletheia*) carries the sense of reality and integrity, reminding believers that spiritual readiness begins with authenticity before God.[105]

Next is the breastplate of righteousness.[106] Made of leather or metal, the Roman soldier's breastplate

---

[104] G225, *alētheia* (ἀλήθεια): carries the sense of truth as reality and integrity, beyond mere factual correctness. In Ephesians, it is more than factual accuracy; *alētheia* is the lived reality of God revealed in Christ, calling believers to integrity, honesty, and alignment with reality as God sees it, not as they perceive it.

[105] Spiros Zodhiates, ed., *Hebrew-Greek Key Word Study Bible* (Chattanooga, TN: AMG Publishers, 2014), "ἀλήθεια."

[106] G1343, *dikaiosynē* (δικαιοσύνη): denotes conformity to God's standard of what is right, both in status before Him and in lived practice.

protected the heart and lungs. Righteousness guards our inner life. Habitual obedience and right living shield the very core of who we are spiritually.[107] Without truth and righteousness, the fight is lost before it begins.

A soldier's sandals were studded with nails for grip, like cleats, so he could stand firm even on rough terrain. Paul says our footing comes from "the readiness given by the gospel of peace" (6:15). The peace of Christ steadies us when the enemy tries to trip us with conflict, anxiety, or discouragement. Even on slippery ground, the gospel keeps us standing.[108]

Then comes the shield of faith. A Roman shield was nearly the size of a door, layered with leather. Some historians suggest that the leather covering may have been treated or even soaked to help extinguish flaming arrows.[109] So too, faith absorbs the enemy's attacks, lies, temptations, accusations, and shame. Faith does not erase the attack, but it renders it powerless. Paul emphasizes that faith is not a vague optimism but a resolute trust in God's promises, able to extinguish the enemy's fiercest attacks.[110]

For the Roman soldier, the helmet, made of iron or bronze, was an extremely strong protection for the

---

107 Bratcher and Nida, *Handbook on Ephesians*, 161.

108 H. D. M. Spence-Jones and Joseph S. Exell, eds., *Ephesians*, The Pulpit Commentary (London; New York: Funk & Wagnalls Company, 1909), 259.

109 Adrian Goldsworthy, *The Complete Roman Army* (London: Thames & Hudson, 2003), 129.

110 Hoehner, "Ephesians," 641–42.

head and neck.[111] For believers, this is about remembering who we are and whose we are. We belong to Christ. We've been rescued from sin and death. We are already citizens of His kingdom, even as we await the final day when salvation will be fully realized. This "already and not yet" tension means we fight with present assurance and future hope. When we wear this salvation identity daily, we walk into battle with confidence, not fear.

Finally, Paul points to the one offensive weapon: "the sword of the Spirit, which is the word of God" (6:17).[112] The short Roman sword was used in close combat, both for defense and counterattack. Likewise, Scripture is both shield and weapon. When we take the Word into our hearts, it becomes the tool by which we resist, fight back, and reclaim ground for the kingdom.

Truth and righteousness, peace and faith, salvation and Scripture—these are our weapons. Paul hints at a deeper sustaining force holding it all together: prayer. Prayer strengthens every piece of our armor, keeps us aligned with God's will, and sustains us in His service.

This is not playacting. The enemy does not surrender easily. He will oppose every attempt to live

---

111 Knowles, Andrew, ed. *The Bible Guide* (Minneapolis, MN: Augsburg Fortress, 2001), 622.

112 G4487, *rhēma* (ῥῆμα): emphasizes the spoken, active Word of God, applied in specific situations. In the context of spiritual warfare, Paul highlights not just the existence of God's Word (*logos*), but the believer wielding God's truth in specific battles of life.

in the light and walk in love. But by the grace of Jesus and the strength of the Spirit, we can stand firm.

Max Anders captures the sense of this passage well: we are to "rest in the finished work of Christ." Satan hisses, "You hypocrite. You're unworthy. You have no right to speak of forgiveness." And we are prone to believe him. But we do not withstand Satan's accusations because of what we do. We withstand Satan's accusations through what Christ has already done on the cross. Resting there, we can resist every scheme, every lie, every attempt to bury us in guilt and shame.[113]

So, when the devil tempts, accuses, or shames you, do not listen. *Stand firm in Christ.* "Be strong in the Lord and in the strength of His might. Put on the full armor of God so that you may be able to stand" (Eph. 6:11).

Spiritual Practice: Suit Up in Prayer

Each morning this week, before checking your phone or turning on the news, pray through the armor of God. Speak it aloud or write it down as a declaration of faith and readiness. "Today, Lord:

- I fasten on the belt of truth. Help me walk in honesty and integrity.
- I put on the breastplate of righteousness. Guard my heart and guide me to choose what is good and right.

---

[113] Anders, *Galatians, Ephesians, Philippians, Colossians*, 193–195.

- I fit my feet with the readiness of the gospel of peace. Wherever I go, let me carry Your peace.
- I take up the shield of faith. Help me trust You when fear, doubt, or temptation strike.
- I put on the helmet of salvation. Remind me that I am Yours, rescued, beloved, and secure.
- I take up the sword of the Spirit, Your Word. Let Scripture shape my thoughts and direct my actions."

End your prayer by asking:

- Where do I need to stand firm today?
- Then carry that awareness with you into the day.

Praying the Message

Mighty God, thank You for the armor You provide. Help us stand firm, not in fear but in faith. Teach us to recognize the real enemy and resist with truth, righteousness, peace, faith, salvation, and Your Word. When the enemy accuses or tempts, remind us of Christ's finished work. Keep us strong in Your might and steady in Your grace. In Jesus's name, Amen.

Further Reflection:

Ephesians 6:10-17

1. **Context Connection**
   Paul closes his letter with a call to "stand firm" in the strength of the Lord. Spiritual warfare, as James Emery White notes, is often less about dramatic encounters and more about the subtle pressures of temptation, compromise, confusion, guilt, shame, and fear.[114] The aim of the enemy is to keep us from living fully for Christ, but God equips us with armor to resist.

   - Which piece of the armor do you feel most confident in right now? Which feels most vulnerable or neglected?
   - How does Paul's image of armor help you think differently about daily spiritual challenges?

2. **Key Themes in the Text**
   The armor of God is not about fighting in our own strength but about wearing the truth, righteousness, peace, faith, salvation, and the Word of God that Christ has already secured for us.

---

[114] James Emery White, *Serious Times: Making Your Life Matter in an Urgent Day* (Downers Grove, IL: InterVarsity Press, 2004), 153.

- How have you experienced the enemy's "breath on your neck"[115] in recent days or seasons?
- How might truth, righteousness, or faith protect you in that situation?

3. **Church and Community Application**
   Sometimes we misidentify the real enemy, turning our frustration toward people rather than the spiritual forces at work. This can damage relationships and divide the church.
   - Think about a time you misidentified the real enemy. How did it affect your response?
   - How can members of a church community help one another see clearly and stand firm together?
4. **Personal Transformation**
   Standing firm is not about fear or bravado but about quiet courage grounded in Christ's victory.
   - What practices or truths help keep you rooted when spiritual battles arise?
   - Where might God be inviting you to strengthen your defenses today?
5. **Closing Blessing or Prayer Prompt**
   Lord, clothe me in Your armor today. Guard my mind, strengthen my faith, and steady my steps in

[115] White, *Serious Times*, 153.

Your peace. Help me stand firm in Your victory and resist every scheme of the enemy.

CHAPTER 10

INCORRUPTIBLE LOVE: PRAYERFULLY EMBODYING THE CHURCH EPHESIANS 6:18–23

Peace be to the brothers, and love with faith, from God the Father and the Lord Jesus Christ. Grace be with all who love our Lord Jesus Christ with love incorruptible.
(Ephesians 6:23–24)

Today, when pastors can't be in the room, they stream a sermon on YouTube or send a text message of encouragement. Paul had none of that. All he had was a pen, parchment, and prayer. And somehow, that was more than enough: not just for his day, but for ours.

As we've studied Ephesians, we've drawn parallels between our own struggles to live out the faith in difficult seasons and the challenges faced by the believers in and around Ephesus and by Paul himself. As we reach the close of this letter, which has been read and cherished in churches around the world for nearly two thousand years, we are reminded of the difficult circumstances under which it was written. Paul composed this message from confinement, and yet it so powerfully summarizes the gospel and its transforming impact on our lives.

This sermon-letter first reached the churches of Asia Minor, and now it reaches us from the heart of a pastor and missionary who described himself as an "ambassador in chains" (6:20). Though called to carry the gospel freely, Paul wrote these words from Roman house arrest. N.T. Wright captures the irony with vivid pictures: an eagle with clipped wings, a great liner stranded in the Sahara, a basketball player bound at the ankles, a train stuck in a ploughed field.

Wright continues: "An ambassador ought to be free to come and go, to take the message of his king wherever it is needed. How can he do that if they've tied him up? These powerful metaphors help us feel the weight of Paul's situation as we come to the end of Ephesians: … the eagle is determined to fly, the liner to sail again come what may. Paul will go on announcing the good news of King Jesus even from a prison cell … But how will he find the right words to say? How will he make the message clear? How will he be able to wrap his own mind sufficiently around the extraordinary saving plan of God and then describe it in such a way that other people will find it convincing and compelling?"[116]

If ever there was a man who had every reason to throw up his arms in defeat, it was the one who wrote the message we've been studying. Since surrendering to the gospel, Paul had been insulted, slandered, beaten, stoned, and left for dead. He longed to be with these struggling believers, to strengthen them in their faith, walk with them through their hardships, and pray alongside them. Instead, he found himself chained to a Roman soldier, with no possibility of connection through a YouTube service, Zoom call, phone, email, or text.

Rather than wallow in pity, Paul picked up his pen and strengthened the church. Even in prison, likely facing execution, Paul clung to his love for the churches and, more importantly, to his love for God. He was able to do that because the gospel wasn't just something Paul preached; it was something he had internalized. He carried the good news and its ministry with him into every circumstance.

The message of Ephesians has been about sharing with the churches in and around Ephesus, and now with us, what Paul already had. This circular letter is about getting the church inside you...inside us.

---

116 Wright, *Paul for Everyone, 77.*

A Life of Prayer

Internalizing the gospel is possible only through a life of prayer. It is fitting that a prayer-soaked letter ends with both an exhortation to pray and a personal request for prayer. From start to finish, this message has been grounded in prayer, with Paul's own prayerfulness often bubbling over as he writes.[117] Everything this epistle teaches about faith and life is ultimately wrapped in the language of prayer.[118]

Paul just wrote about putting on the armor of God. Here, we are reminded that prayer is the energy that enables the Christian soldier to stand firm, to wear the armor, and to wield the sword. We cannot fight life's spiritual battles in our own strength, no matter how gifted or determined we think we are.[119] That is why Paul does not end the letter without urging us to pray constantly.[120] In just a few verses, he uses various words for prayer six times.[121] To prepare for and engage in spiritual warfare, we must stay alert and prayerful, crying out to God for our own needs and for the needs of the saints.

---

[117] Dockery, "The Pauline Letters," 580.

[118] Peterson, *Practice Resurrection*, Kindle Page 3058.

[119] Warren W. Wiersbe, *The Bible Exposition Commentary*, vol. 2 (Wheaton, IL: Victor Books, 1996), 59.

[120] Bratcher and Nida, *Handbook on Ephesians*, 164.

[121] G4336, *Proseuchomai* (προσεύχομαι): the most common New Testament word for prayer, meaning "to lift our desires toward God." G1162, *Deēsis* (δέησις): carries the sense of urgent pleading from a place of need. Paul uses both in this passage.

Christians are to remain attentive to the battle, in constant communication with our commanding Lord, and faithfully supporting our fellow soldiers.[122] In verse 18 alone, the Greek word for "all" or "every" appears four times.[123] Prayer for everything and everyone is the heartbeat of a life filled with the church.[124]

We might ask when we should pray or what we should pray for, and Paul's answer would simply be, "Yes, pray always, in every way, for all things, and for all people."

Paul also modeled the humility of asking for prayer. He asked that others would pray for him so that he could find courage to keep proclaiming the gospel even from prison. I always appreciated how my late friend Charles Armstrong approached this. So many of us are too proud to admit our need, but Charles would say, "Brother, if I have a need in my life, I'm going to let the church know." That kind of honesty is a gift to the church.

My hunch is that more of us would find the strength and spiritual depth we need to stay faithful in hard seasons if we practiced that kind of humility, if we simply said, "While you are praying for all the saints, do not forget to pray for me. I could really use it this

---

122 Knowles, *The Bible Guide*, 622.

123 G3956, *pas* (πᾶς): translated "all" or "every," occurs four times in Ephesians 6:18, underscoring the comprehensiveness of prayer: all prayer, all times, all perseverance, all saints.

124 Liefeld, *Ephesians*, Eph. 6:18–20.

week." If we could get over ourselves enough to be honest about our struggles and ask one another for prayer, I think we would be amazed at the difference that kind of shared life of prayer could make.

Paul had already settled in his heart that he would keep speaking about King Jesus, His victory over death, and His kingdom now breaking into the world, no matter what happened. But he also knew he could only do that effectively if the church was praying for him.[125] How much more could we accomplish for God's kingdom if we remembered that?

Eugene Peterson reminds us that the call to "pray at all times in the Spirit" means far more than simply saying prayers. As we mature in Christ and get His church inside us, prayer becomes the language that undergirds and flows through all we say and do.

"Not all prayers are conscious," Peterson writes. "Not all prayers can be identified as prayers. Prayer is the language underlying and sometimes surfacing in all our language as we grow up in Christ. Most of us pray a good deal more than we are aware that we are praying." As we saturate our lives in prayer, it undergirds all that we say and do until it becomes as natural as conversing with a friend or even breathing.

Prayer is not a performance or a skill we master by trying harder. It is a language we grow into as we fill our lives with Scripture and deepen our fellowship with

---

125 Wright, *Paul for Everyone*, 77.

God's people. And it does not always look or sound religious. Peterson says we are often praying and learning to pray even when we are not aware of it: when we are listening to Scripture, worshiping together, or simply living in step with God's Spirit. Prayer becomes the language of ongoing communion with God, quietly flowing beneath the surface of all of life.[126]

Prayer is the believer's living, breathing way of life. When I drive my boys to school in the mornings and we pray together for the day ahead, we are living in prayer. When I meet with friends, colleagues, or church members and we laugh together, talk about life, or sometimes cry together, these seasons of fellowship often grow out of prayer or lead into prayer. When a dear friend sends out a group message and we reply with spiritual encouragement, praying hands, and Scripture, we are living in prayer. While fellowship and prayer are distinct practices, Paul's vision of a life "praying in the Spirit at all times" suggests that every act of fellowship can become prayerful when it is lived in conscious communion with God.

People often ask me for prayer. When someone does this, I do my best to stop whatever we are doing, join hands, and pray for whatever this person is facing. This discipline helps me remember and, hopefully, models that prayer should always be welcome in the life of a believer, less like an event to attend and more like

---

[126] Peterson, *Practice Resurrection*, Kindle Page 3076–79.

an ongoing conversation with God that underlies all we say and do.

Prayer is a reminder that God is at work in our story and we are participants in His. These moments root us in His unfolding drama. When our lives become saturated with prayer, it permeates everything we do and shapes who we are. That was enough to change the world in Paul's day, and it still is enough today.

Spiritual Practice: Embodying the Idea of the Church Through Prayer

This week, practice prayerful presence. Set aside time each day to pray for someone in your church and then reach out with a word of encouragement (just a text, a call, or a handwritten note). Ask for prayer yourself.

Choose one person and say, "Would you pray for me this week?" Let your life echo Paul's, who prayed for the saints even in chains, and who had the humility to ask for prayer himself.

Here's one simple rhythm you could follow:

- **Monday:** Pray for someone by name and send a quick message of encouragement.
- **Tuesday:** Ask a trusted friend to pray for you.
- **Wednesday:** Whisper breath prayers throughout the day ("Lord, give me peace… Jesus, guide my words…"). A breath prayer is a simple, Scripture-shaped phrase repeated in rhythm with your breathing to stay aware of

God's presence. It's a way of letting prayer become as natural as breathing.

- **Thursday:** Look for a moment of spiritual conversation, a doorway to talk about faith.
- **Friday:** End the week by naming where you saw God at work and giving thanks.

This is how the church grows inside us: not only through sermons and theology but through daily prayers, shared burdens, and real conversations with real people. Prayer does not float in abstraction; it takes root in fellowship. The very prayers Paul requested would be carried on the lips of friends like Tychicus.

A Shared Life of Faith

That kind of prayerful, faith-internalizing life naturally grows out of fellowship. Ephesians differs from many of Paul's other New Testament writings because it lacks the personal notes we are accustomed to finding in his correspondence. If we received a message today that sounded like Paul's other New Testament letters, we might find things like, "Don't forget to tell the Cortez and Jones families I said, 'hi,'" or "Please tell David Mata and Mark Garza to behave." Those little touches remind us that Paul's theology is always grounded in real relationships, with specific people in specific places.

Ephesians, by contrast, reads more like a circular sermon, probably intended to be read aloud in multiple churches. It is less localized, more universal. And yet, even here, at the close of this sweeping letter, Paul wraps things up with a very personal note, reminding us that doctrine is never divorced from relationship.

> *So that you also may know how I am and what I am doing, Tychicus the beloved brother and faithful minister in the Lord will tell you everything. I have sent him to you for this very purpose, that you may know how we are, and that he may encourage your hearts* (6:21–22).

Even in this general, all-church message, Paul reminds us that the gospel is always lived out in relationship, with God and with one another. We do not internalize the church by ourselves. We live it together, through friendship, encouragement, and a shared life in the Spirit.

Having shown us how prayer roots the church inside us, Paul also reminds us, through Tychicus, that the church is always embodied in people.

Tychicus: A Trusted Messenger

These final verses include a practical note, almost identical to one in Colossians, reminding us that Paul likely wrote that specific letter and this more general one at the same time while under house arrest, sending both with Tychicus for delivery.[127]

Paul was, quite literally, tied up. He could not travel to visit these churches, drop off his letters at a local delivery service, or attach his letters to an email. The

---

[127]Wright, *Paul for Everyone*, 79.

only way to get this message to its intended audience was to send it by hand with a trusted friend and colleague.

Tychicus was that kind of friend. We do not know much about him, but he appears several times in the New Testament as a reliable, appreciated servant of the Lord with ties to the Ephesian church.[128] We can carry God's message in the same spirit today. Every text, visit, or casserole left on a doorstep is a little Tychicus moment, reminding us that doors are opened to the gospel not just in sermons, but in embodied love.

Paul describes him as a "beloved brother"[129] and a "faithful minister."[130] These words carry weight. The first speaks of someone deeply loved, the same word

---

[128] Liefeld, *Ephesians*, Eph 6:21–24

[129] G27, G80, agapētos adelphos (ἀγαπητὸς ἀδελφός): beloved brother. *Agapētos* comes from *agapaō* ("to love deeply, sacrificially"), used often of God's love for Jesus (Matt. 3:17) and of believers as "beloved in the Lord." It conveys more than affection; it means being embraced by God's covenant love. *Adelphos* literally means "from the same womb," used for both physical and spiritual siblings. Here it highlights the family bond believers share in Christ.

[130] G4103, G1249, *pistos diakonos (*πιστὸς διάκονος): faithful minister or servant. *Pistos* denotes trustworthiness and reliability. It describes someone proven over time. Often translated "faithful," the word can convey the idea of loyal reliability or trustworthy devotion. *Diakonos* literally refers to a servant or attendant, one who carries out service on behalf of another, and came to describe those engaged in ministry or practical service (the root of our word *deacon*). Paul often applies it to gospel workers who embody servant-leadership (cf. 1 Cor. 3:5).

Paul often uses for believers who are beloved in Christ. The second emphasizes reliability, trustworthiness, and steady devotion. The word translated *minister* points to servant leadership, ministry expressed in practical service. Tychicus was not only dependable; he embodied the gospel by the way he served.

While introducing Tychicus as the courier certainly serves a practical purpose, it also adds something deeply personal. Paul makes it clear that the resurrection life he describes is not abstract theology. It is a personal life, lived in real places, among specific people.

The role Tychicus plays reminds us that this was not just a message to be studied; it was a message meant to be shared. Tychicus would not simply hand over a scroll. He would bring personal updates: news of Paul's imprisonment, his fears, his hopes, and his steadfast trust in Christ. He would offer stories about the gospel's progress, the challenges facing the church in Rome, and the work God was doing throughout the world.

Tychicus did not just deliver a message. He embodied it. Tychicus carried the gospel with grace, presence, and peace. In a world full of chaos and spiritual battle, sometimes encouragement is the very thing we need most.

Peterson beautifully captures the depth of what Tychicus represents. Tychicus is the only person Paul mentions by name in Ephesians, not counting references to himself. Like the eighty personal names Paul mentions in his other letters, here Tychicus' name links

> *the message of the gospel to a particular man or woman growing up in Christ, practicing resurrection while working for a living, raising a family, dealing with whatever political and economic conditions impinged on his or her life. Every word written on these pages has been lived—not just written or preached or taught or discussed, but lived in real-world conditions with all the factors of those conditions at play.*[131]

Peterson continues, reminding us that church is not an abstraction or a program to manage. It is a gift. The church is a living community where we learn to practice resurrection in real life, through real people. Church happens in the conversations between God and the people He names, people like Tychicus, people like us. Church is not limited to sermons, meetings, or mission statements. It is found in names, meals, small talk, and shared sorrows.[132]

The news Tychicus brought to these churches of Asia Minor was more than information. Paul's statement that Tychicus would "tell you everything" (v. 21) referred specifically to news about the apostle's own life and ministry.[133] The way Tychicus would share

---

131 Peterson, *Practice Resurrection*, Kindle Page 3110–20.

132 Ibid.

133 G3956, *panta* (πάντα): "*everything, all things*." A comprehensive word, from the root *pas* ("all, every"), often used by Paul to emphasize the sweeping scope of God's work.

it, through his presence, his encouragement, and his faithfulness, embodied the message itself. In the same way, every time we share the good news of Jesus, every encouragement we offer, and every act of presence and prayer can help make the church real in our own time.

Flesh-and-blood saints like Tychicus help us see that ordinary people like us really can get the church inside us when we live together in prayerful, faithful community.

Peace, Love, Faith, Grace

Paul's final words echo his very first. Ephesians began with an invitation to share in God's grace and peace (1:2), and it ends with the same blessing. This is a literary inclusio, framing the whole letter in God's unearned favor and reconciling peace. What began with grace and peace now closes with "peace,"[134] "love,"[135]

---

[134]G1515, *eirēnē* (εἰρήνη): *"peace."* More than the absence of conflict, eirēnē carries the sense of wholeness, harmony, and well-being. It parallels the Hebrew *shalom*, often used in greetings and blessings to describe God's order restoring creation. As Paul concludes this letter, *peace* reflects the unity Christ secured between God and humanity and among believers themselves, a wholeness that holds the community together in love.

[135] G26: *agape*, (ἀγάπη): "love." Distinct from affection (*philia*) or desire (*eros*), *agapē* denotes sacrificial, covenantal love. It is the love God shows in Christ (John 3:16) and the love poured into believers' hearts by the Spirit (Rom. 5:5). In Paul's closing words, *love* joined "with faith" reflects the self-giving love that unites believers in Christ and sustains the life of the church.

"faith,"[136] and "grace,"[137] reminding us that the Christian life both starts and ends in the gifts of God.

Mark Roberts summed it up well: "The letter began with God choosing us before the foundation of the world. It ends with the hope of an endless future, one that is indeed filled with God's grace for us and our love for Christ."[138]

In a world marked by conflict, hatred, and strife, the message of the church is this: we can have peace with God and peace with one another across every barrier that once divided us. To people starving for acceptance and affection, always feeling the need to prove themselves worthy, the church proclaims that we are recipients of the unconditional love of our Creator, made accessible through faith alone.

These gifts are ours, not because we have earned them, but because we have encountered the grace of

---

136 G4102, *pistis* (πίστις): "faith, trust, belief." At root, *pistis* is trust or confidence. In Paul's writings, it refers both to trusting God personally and to the body of truth Christians believe. It conveys reliance rather than mere intellectual assent. In this passage, *faith* expresses steadfast trust in God that anchors believers in Christ and binds them together in loyal dependence on Him.

137 G5485, *charis* (χάρις): "grace, favor, gift." *Charis* signifies God's unmerited favor freely given to His people. In Greek culture, it referred to generosity or goodwill shown without obligation. For Paul, *grace* is God's initiating love that saves and sustains believers apart from works (Eph. 2:8). Here, at the close of Ephesians, *grace* conveys God's enduring favor resting upon all who love Christ with undying devotion.

138 Roberts, *Ephesians*, 257.

Almighty God. That is what it means to internalize the gospel, to live with the church growing inside of us. That message cannot be snuffed out by persecution, isolation, illness, or anything else life may bring.

That is the heart of Ephesians. That is the calling of the church.

> *Peace be to the brothers, and love with faith, from God the Father and the Lord Jesus Christ. Grace be with all who love our Lord Jesus Christ with love incorruptible.* (6:23–24)

This is what it means to get the church inside you: to live a life wrapped in grace and peace, grounded in faith and love, until Christ's presence shapes every part of who you are.

Praying the Message:

Lord Jesus, You have called us into a life of prayer and fellowship, where Your church takes root in our hearts and overflows through our lives. Teach us to pray in the Spirit, to lift one another up, and to live with honesty and grace. Make us faithful messengers of Your gospel, carrying peace, love, and encouragement wherever we go. Give us a love that endures, a love that is incorruptible and never fading, and bring Your church to life in us. Amen.

Further Reflection

Ephesians 6:18–23

1. **Context Connection**
   Paul closes his letter urging believers to pray "at all times in the Spirit" and to pray "also for me." He knows the gospel moves forward not just through preaching but through the unseen ministry of prayer. This final section reminds us that the life of the church is sustained and strengthened when believers pray for one another.

   - How does Paul's request for prayer model humility and dependence on the body of Christ?
   - How might asking others to pray for you help your church grow in strength and maturity?

2. **Key Themes in the Text**
   Persistent prayer connects us to God's power and to one another. Paul highlights prayer as a central work of the church, not an optional extra.

   - How would you describe your current prayer life for others in your church?
   - How might you begin or renew a rhythm of praying for others and asking for prayer yourself?

3. **Church and Community Application**
   When prayer becomes a shared rhythm, the

church becomes a place where no one stands alone.

- What would it look like for your church to be marked by this kind of prayerful presence?
- Who might God be prompting you to intercede for this week?

4. **Personal Transformation**
   Living with the church inside us means weaving prayer into the ordinary moments of life and letting the Spirit shape our relationships through intercession.

   - What daily habits could you adopt to pray more intentionally for others?
   - How can you make space to listen for God's voice in prayer?

5. **Closing Blessing or Prayer Prompt**
   This is the incorruptible love that holds us, sustains us, and calls us to live as Christ's church in the world.

Epilogue

Let the Church Live Inside You

"Peace be to the brothers, and love with faith, from God the Father and the Lord Jesus Christ. Grace be with all who love our Lord Jesus Christ with love incorruptible" (Ephesians 6:23–24).

What the world needs most is not simply a stronger church organization but a deeper church presence, a presence that takes shape in grace-filled relationships, everyday obedience, and gospel-shaped living. This work begins personally and quietly in the heart of each believer and in communities gathered for worship, fellowship, and service to others.

As we close, may Peterson's rendering of Paul's words be a blessing over you. May they draw you more deeply into the life of Christ's church until it lives fully inside of you:

"Good-bye, friends. Love mixed with faith be yours from God the Father and from the Master, Jesus Christ. Pure grace and nothing but grace be with all who love our Master, Jesus Christ."[139]

Amen.

[139] Eugene H. Peterson, *The Message: The Bible in Contemporary Language* (Colorado Springs: NavPress, 2005), Eph 6:23–24.

BIBLIOGRAPHY

Allen, Catherine B. *The New Lottie Moon Story*. Nashville, TN: Broadman Press, 1980.

Anders, Max. *Galatians, Ephesians, Philippians, Colossians*. Vol. 8 of *Holman New Testament Commentary*. Nashville, TN: Broadman & Holman Publishers, 1999.

Arnold, Clinton E. *Ephesians*. Vol. 10 of Zondervan Exegetical Commentary on the New Testament. Grand Rapids, MI: Zondervan, 2010.

Barclay, William. *The Letters to the Galatians and Ephesians*. The New Daily Study Bible. Louisville, KY, London: Westminster John Knox Press, 2002.

Baudelaire, Charles. *Paris Spleen, 1869*. Translated by Louise Varèse. New York: New Directions, 1970.

Bond, J. B. "The Epistle of Paul the Apostle to the Ephesians." In *The Grace New Testament Commentary*, edited by Robert N. Wilkin. Denton, TX: Grace Evangelical Society, 2010.

Bratcher, Robert G., and Eugene A. Nida. *A Handbook on Paul's Letter to the Ephesians*. New York: United Bible Societies, 1993.

Carson, D. A., R. T. France, J. A. Motyer, and Gordon J. Wenham, eds. *New Bible Commentary: 21st Century Edition*. 4th ed. Leicester, England, Downers Grove, IL: InterVarsity Press, 1994.

Cloud, Henry, and John Townsend. *Boundaries: When to Say Yes, How to Say No to Take*

Control of Your Life. Grand Rapids, MI: Zondervan, 1992.

Cohick, Lynn. *Ephesians: A New Covenant Commentary*. Eugene, OR: Cascade Books,

2010.

Crabb, Larry. *Inside Out.* Colorado Springs: NavPress, 1988.

Dockery, David S. "The Pauline Letters." In *Holman Concise Bible Commentary*, edited by David S. Dockery. Nashville, TN: Broadman & Holman Publishers, 1998.

Donelson, Lewis. *Colossians, Ephesians, 1 and 2 Timothy, and Titus*. Louisville, KY: Westminster John Knox Press, 1996.

Easton, M. G. *Illustrated Bible Dictionary and Treasury of Biblical History, Biography, Geography, Doctrine, and Literature*. New York, 1893.

Erickson, Millard J. "Ephesians." In *The Evangelical Commentary on the Bible*, edited by Walter A. Elwell. Grand Rapids, MI: Baker Book House, 1989.

Fields, W. C. "Ephesians." In *The Teacher's Bible Commentary: A Concise, Thorough Interpretation of the Entire Bible Designed Especially for Sunday School Teachers*, edited by H. Franklin Paschall and Herschel H. Hobbs. Nashville, TN: Broadman and Holman Publishers, 1972.

Foulkes, Francis. *Ephesians: An Introduction and Commentary*. Tyndale New Testament Commentaries, vol. 10. Downers Grove: InterVarsity Press, 1989.

Goldsworthy, Adrian. *The Complete Roman Army*. London: Thames & Hudson, 2003.

Hoehner, Harold W. "Ephesians." In *The Bible Knowledge Commentary: An Exposition of the Scriptures*, edited by J. F.

Walvoord and R. B. Zuck. Vol. 2. Wheaton, IL: Victor Books, 1985.

Hoehner, Harold W. *Ephesians: An Exegetical Commentary*. Grand Rapids, MI: Baker Academic, 2002.

Jordan, Clarence. *The Cotton Patch Gospel*. Macon, GA: Smyth & Helwys Publishing, 2004.

Keel, Othmar. *The Symbolism of the Biblical World: Ancient Near Eastern Iconography and the*

Book of Psalms. Translated by Timothy J. Hallett. Winona Lake: Eisenbrauns, 1997.

Keener, Craig S. *The IVP Bible Background Commentary: New Testament*. Downers Grove: InterVarsity Press, 1993.

Keller, Timothy. *The Meaning of Marriage: Facing the Complexities of Commitment with the Wisdom of God*. New York: Dutton, 2011.

Kimmel, Tim. *Grace-Based Parenting*. Nashville, TN: Thomas Nelson, 2005.

King, Martin Luther, Jr. *Strength to Love*. New York: Harper & Row, 1963.

Knowles, Andrew, ed. *The Bible Guide*. 1st Augsburg books ed. Minneapolis: Augsburg, 2001.

Liddell, Henry George, Robert Scott, and Henry Stuart Jones. *A Greek-English Lexicon*. Oxford: Clarendon Press, 1996.

Liefeld, Walter L. *Ephesians*. The IVP New Testament Commentary Series, vol. 10. Downers Grove, IL: InterVarsity Press, 1997.

Mare, W. Harold. *New Testament Background Commentary: A New Dictionary of Words, Phrases and Situations in Bible Order.* Fearn, Scotland: Mentor, 2004.

McKnight, Scot. *Ephesians and Colossians: Diversity in Unity.* New Testament Everyday Bible Study Series. Grand Rapids, MI: HarperChristian Resources, 2025.

McKnight, Scot. *The King Jesus Gospel: The Original Good News Revisited.* Grand Rapids: Zondervan, 2011.

Moon, Lottie. *Send the Light: Lottie Moon's Letters and Other Writings.* Edited by Keith Harper. Macon, GA: Mercer University Press, 2002.

Muddiman, John. *The Epistle to the Ephesians.* Black's New Testament Commentary. London: Continuum, 2001.

O'Brien, Peter Thomas. *The Letter to the Ephesians.* The Pillar New Testament Commentary. Grand Rapids, MI: W.B. Eerdmans Publishing Co., 1999.

Peterson, Eugene H. *The Invitation: A Simple Guide to the Bible.* Colorado Springs, CO: NavPress, 2008.

Peterson, Eugene H. *The Jesus Way: A Conversation on the Ways That Jesus Is the Way.* Grand Rapids, MI: Eerdmans, 2007.

Peterson, Eugene H. *The Message: The Bible in Contemporary Language.* Colorado Springs: NavPress, 2005.

Peterson, Eugene H. *Practice Resurrection: A Conversation on Growing Up in Christ.* Grand Rapids, MI: William B. Eerdmans Publishing Company, 2010.

Rasnake, Eddie. *The Book of Ephesians.* Following God Through the Bible. Chattanooga, TN: AMG Publishers, 2003.

Richards, Lawrence O. *The Bible Reader's Companion.* Electronic ed. Wheaton, IL: Victor Books, 1991.

Roberts, Mark D. *Ephesians.* Edited by Scot McKnight. The Story of God Bible Commentary. Grand Rapids, MI: Zondervan, 2016.

Robertson, A. T. *Word Pictures in the New Testament.* Nashville, TN: Broadman Press, 1933.

Spence-Jones, H. D. M., and Joseph S. Exell, eds. *Ephesians.* The Pulpit Commentary. New York: Funk & Wagnalls Company, 1909.

Sproul, R. C. *The Purpose of God: Ephesians.* Scotland: Christian Focus Publications, 1994.

Stott, John. *Romans: God's Good News for the World.* Downers Grove: InterVarsity Press, 1994.

Strong, James. *The Exhaustive Concordance of the Bible.* New York: Hunt and Eaton; Cincinnati: Cranston and Curts, 1890.

Summers, Ray. "Ephesians, Letter to The." In *Holman Illustrated Bible Dictionary*, edited by Chad Brand et al., 491. Nashville, TN: Holman Bible Publishers, 2015.

Turner, Max. "Ephesians." In *New Bible Commentary: 21st Century Edition*, 4th ed., edited by D. A. Carson et al., 1243. Leicester, England; Downers Grove, IL: InterVarsity Press, 1994.

Utley, Robert James. *Paul Bound, the Gospel Unbound: Letters from Prison (Colossians, Ephesians and Philemon, Then Later, Philippians).* Vol. 8 of *Study Guide Commentary Series.* Marshall, TX: Bible Lessons International, 1997.

Walvoord, John F., and Roy B. Zuck, eds. *The Bible Knowledge Commentary: An Exposition of the Scriptures*. 2 vols. Wheaton, IL: Victor Books, 1985.

White, James Emery. *Serious Times: Making Your Life Matter in an Urgent Day*. Downers

Grove, IL: InterVarsity Press, 2004.

Wiersbe, Warren W. *The Bible Exposition Commentary*, vol. 2. Wheaton, IL: Victor Books, 1996.

Wilkin, Robert N., ed. *The Grace New Testament Commentary*. Denton, TX: Grace Evangelical Society, 2010.

Wright, N.T. *Paul for Everyone: The Prison Letters—Ephesians, Philippians, Colossians, and Philemon*. London: Society for Promoting Christian Knowledge, 2004.

Wright, N. T. *Surprised by Hope: Rethinking Heaven, the Resurrection, and the Mission of the Church*. New York: HarperOne, 2008.

Wuest, Kenneth S. *Wuest's Word Studies from the Greek New Testament: For the English Reader*. Vol. 1. Grand Rapids: Eerdmans, 1973.

Zodhiates, Spiros, ed. *Hebrew-Greek Key Word Study Bible: ESV Edition*. Revised ed. Chattanooga, TN: AMG Publishers, 2014.

For additional resources and information on upcoming projects from Steven K. Parker, log onto

https://www.drstevenparker.com.

About Kharis Publishing:

Kharis Publishing, an imprint of Kharis Media LLC, is a leading Christian and inspirational book publisher based in Aurora, Chicago metropolitan area, Illinois. Kharis' dual mission is to give voice to under-represented writers (including women and first-time authors) and equip orphans in developing countries with literacy tools. That is why, for each book sold, the publisher channels some of the proceeds into providing books and computers for orphanages in developing countries so that these kids may learn to read, dream, and grow. For a limited time, Kharis Publishing is accepting unsolicited queries for nonfiction (Christian, self-help, memoirs, business, health and wellness) from qualified leaders, professionals, pastors, and ministers. Learn more at: https://kharispublishing.com/

www.ingramcontent.com/pod-product-compliance
Lightning Source LLC
La Vergne TN
LVHW010614100826
845148LV00014B/2970

* 9 7 8 1 6 3 7 4 6 6 7 5 9 *